Becoming A Wealth Creator

Advancing into Kingdom Prosperity

BARBARA WENTROBLE

FOREWORD

For thousands of years the majority of Christians have functioned under a great misunderstanding about the purpose of wealth, primarily because they believe it is somehow more "blessed to be poor" than be wealthy. This is a major misinterpretation of God's will for His people.

I do not see anywhere throughout scripture that God wants His people to be financially poor. He wants His people to flourish to be witnesses to the unbeliever. Wealth is a witness for God to unbelievers when they see a humble and generous heart.

We fulfill God's command to advance the Kingdom on Earth by evangelizing, but we are also called to provide for the needs of others whether by our tithes and offerings or tangible goods.

The poor cannot provide for the poor. They cannot give what they do not have to give; food, clothing, and shelter typically cost money.

God wants His people to have more than enough so they can bless others and be a witness to His promises. "They spoke to Moses, saying, 'The people bring much more than enough for the service of the work which the LORD commanded *us* to do'" (Exodus 36:5).

In Genesis 1, God directs His people to be fruitful, increase, and expand throughout Earth. They were to show the goodness of God and to fulfill His covenant. "It is He who give you power to get wealth, that he may establish His covenant" (Deuteronomy

8:18). Why would God go against His own word and expect His people to be poor?

God provides many sources for His people to be creators of wealth and then be stewards of that wealth to advance his Kingdom on Earth. Finances and goods come from the fruit of our labors and the promises and blessings of God. He wants Christians to prosper and be witnesses of a blessed life, but more importantly to advance his Kingdom as distributors of the blessings.

Making money is not the primary thing. It is being able to use money to advance the Kingdom of God. Money is just a tool for Kingdom advancement.

God wants us to do everything with a spirit of excellence and achieve greater things as His witnesses. Many things He is calling us to do can only be accomplished when the finances are available to use.

Every mission trip requires finances. Every building requires finances. Every outreach program requires finances. Life requires finances. An abundant life and an abundant giver require wealth.

The level we choose is the level we attain.
To create wealth in today's marketplace throughout the world requires a much higher level of knowledge, wisdom, and understanding. Wealth Creators not only should gain practical knowledge about finances, businesses, and workplace dynamics but also spiritual knowledge. They should have an understanding about how to be wise in various situations and dealing with the opposition.

I think many Christians make excuses for not becoming a Wealth Creator because they are afraid or unwilling to learn. Fear and laziness stop people from fulfilling their own dreams, but worse, it stops them from fulfilling God's plan for Earth.

God has given "you power to get wealth that he may establish His covenant." Now is the time to grab onto that power and authority from God. Now is the time to learn what He wants you to know to be a successful Wealth Creator!

Now is the time to read Barbara Wentroble's book on *Becoming a Wealth Creator* and receive from her valuable instruction and revelation about God's principles and reasons for establishing wealth.

Wentroble's teaching gift clearly defines a biblical perspective about wealth along with revelational keys from her prophetic gifting to help the reader break old mindsets and establish new ones.

I find this book very practical, and I strongly encourage you to read it! You will be blessed to be a Wealth Creator!

Dr. John P. Kelly
International Convenor of ICAL
International Coalition of Apostolic Leaders

INTRODUCTION

Wealth! That word creates various responses in many different people. When hearing the word, some people respond in joy. They are excited about the possibility of increasing wealth for the future. Other people respond in discouragement. "That can never happen in our family. No one has ever been able to break out of poverty." Others respond in a wistful way but without much hope. "I hope someday I can have a little extra in my bank account."

Wealth for some people is different than wealth for other people. I will never forget my friend Jay Swallow and how he defined wealth. Jay was a powerful Native American apostle. He helped shift people into new levels of freedom. Jay is in Heaven now, but his words are still ringing in my spirit. He boldly spoke: "Wealth to us, Native Americans, is a paved driveway and a one-breed dog." Jay, along with everyone else, laughed when he said this. However, Jay was speaking with truth. For some people having a better living situation in the future would be considered wealth.

What is wealth?
Wealth is merely the abundance of valuable possessions or money. For a billionaire, wealth might be an increase of several billion dollars. For an ordinary citizen in the Western culture, wealth may be the cancellation of debt and an increase of several thousand dollars each year.

I believe the Lord gave me the assignment to write this book to encourage every believer to step into a new level of wealth. A person can follow principles in this book and find themselves breaking out of limitations from the past. Your current financial situation does not exempt you from becoming a Wealth Creator. Your mindset and your connections can limit you!

Mindset limitations
A mindset of poverty has been prevalent in the Church for many years. The poverty mindset sometimes causes Christians to believe they are selfish. To be godly, they should give away all their possessions. They are surely carnal people, or they would fill their home with homeless people. Some believers almost feel guilty if they have a nice home and a good car.

The Lord's promise concerning wealth is a weapon to defeat the mindset of poverty.

> You shall remember the Lord your God, for it is he who is giving you power to make wealth, that He may confirm His covenant which he swore to your fathers, as *it is* this day.
> Deuteronomy 8:18

God is a good father. He wants to do good things for His children. Father God also desires to give His children everything they need to fulfill their assignment on Earth.

Mankind's earthly assignment

Mankind was put on Earth with an assignment from God. They were not placed here to do what I call "breathe in, breath out and wait to go to Heaven." Mankind was given an assignment to increase and to multiply. They were to subdue Earth and make Earth look more like Heaven (Genesis 1:26-28). The Bible reveals mankind failed in his assignment. Man's failure did not stop God's dream.

God sent His own Son, Jesus, to fulfill His dream. God's dream was for a generation of people to arise on Earth. They would enforce the victory of Jesus by overpowering evil forces, defeating Satan's plan for poverty, lack, illness and many other evils. God handed Jesus the keys to bring restoration into the world. Jesus then turned to His followers and handed them the keys. He gave the same command given to Adam and Eve.

> Go therefore and make disciples of all the nations, baptizing them in the name of the Father and the Son and the Holy Spirit, teaching them to observe all that I commanded you; and lo, I am with you always, even to the end of the age.
> Matthew 28:19-20

Wealth for reformation

Wealth is needed for mankind to be obedient to his assignment in the earth. It takes more than lots of churches in a city for the city to be reformed. It takes more than increasing the population of Heaven by converting lots of people to Christianity. All of that is important. However, more is needed.

I live in the Dallas-Fort Worth area of Texas. I read a statistic several years ago about my city. The report stated that Dallas is the most "Christianized" city in the United States. There are more people in my city, per capita, that say they are Christians than any other city. Having more churches and more believers has not reformed Dallas. We still have crime, drugs, murders, human trafficking, and many other evils in our city. God loves my city, and so do I! Changing my city, as well as changing your city, takes lots of finances. Christians must become Wealth Creators to help bring reformation to territories, individuals and their families.

Hope for the future

Ask the Lord to break you out of any limitations that are trying to hold you captive. Believe for a better tomorrow than what you are experiencing today. The Bible records a time when God's people were going into captivity. The city was devastated by the enemy. Yet, God spoke a word of hope to Jeremiah for his future.

> Thou hast said to me, O Lord God, "Buy for yourself the field with money, and call in witnesses" – although the city is given into the hand of the Chaldeans. Then the word of the Lord came to Jeremiah, saying, "Behold, I am the Lord, the God of all flesh; is anything too difficult for Me?"
>
> Jeremiah 32:25-27

God told Jeremiah to buy property in a devasted city. He knew the time would come when the situation would be reversed. The people would return and rebuild the ruins. Buying the field would give Jeremiah hope for his future.

What is one step that you can take to help you have hope for your future as a Wealth Creator? God told Jeremiah that nothing was impossible for Him. That promise is for God's people today. He is the God of all hope. Nothing is impossible for Him. Get ready for a new journey on your path to creating wealth. You have a Kingdom advancing assignment. You were born for this assignment!

DEDICATION

In loving memory of

C. Peter Wagner

C. Peter Wagner changed the Church worldwide and changed the lives of thousands of people around the globe. His humor was his trademark. Peter could not teach a lesson before pulling out a piece of paper, reading the joke and laughing hilariously. The audience laughed along with him. They were not always just laughing at the joke. They were also laughing at Peter enjoying his own joke!

Peter was willing to change his mind as God revealed hidden truths to the Church. He admitted when his doctrine in the past was incomplete and boldly made a stand for "present truth" (2 Peter 1:12). Two of the present truths that Peter endorsed were breaking the spirit of poverty and the transference of wealth. I remind people frequently that Peter encouraged people to create multiple streams of income. He realized it takes finances to advance the Kingdom of God.

My life was impacted in a powerful way through my alignment with Peter. I am sure he is rejoicing in Heaven for the call to all believers to become Wealth Creators.

I am filled with gratitude to C. Peter Wagner as I lovingly dedicate this book to his memory!

CONTENTS

Foreword   i

Introduction   iv

Dedication   ix

1   Should Christians Desire Wealth?   Pg 13

2   Revelation of Biblical Economics   Pg 22

3   Doctrines of Socialism, Communism and Capitalism   Pg 33

4   Biblical Principle of Inheritance   Pg 43

5   Breaking a Poverty Mindset   Pg 53

6   Defeating Debt   Pg 63

7   War Over Wealth   Pg 74

8   Alignment for Wealth Creation   Pg 84

9   Entrepreneurship   Pg 94

10   Giving Unlocks Wealth   Pg 105

11   SMART Goals for Advancing   Pg 117

12   Path to Becoming a Wealth Creator   Pg 127

About the Author   Pg 139

Empowering Resources   Pg 141

CHAPTER 1

Should Christians Desire Wealth?

Meetings with this group of nationally recognized prophets was always exciting! We met a couple times each year to share what we felt the Lord was speaking to the Body of Christ. After a time of prayer, one prophet shared a vision he had while we were praying.

"I saw two angels come into the room. They each brought a basket filled with gold. After putting down the baskets of gold, they left." The prophet did not give the interpretation of the vision. He only shared what he saw with his prophetic eyes.

Others in the room questioned him. "Why did the angels leave two baskets filled with gold?"
The prophet said he had the impression from the Lord that the vision was a picture of the wealth that is coming to the Body of Christ. "Why is the wealth coming at this time?" someone asked. No one had the answer. Through prayer, the group immediately went into the Council Room of the Lord. We wanted to get an answer from the Lord concerning the basketfuls of wealth that the angels had left.

After the prophets spent time in prayer in the Lord's Council Room, the answer came. The prophets all sensed this is the right time for the Lord to release wealth to many in the Body of Christ. The reason for the release of wealth at this time was important. If wealth had been released at an earlier time, many would have spent the money on themselves. The group of prophets sensed many in the Body of Christ had reached maturity. The wealth would now be disbursed for Kingdom purposes and not on selfish desires. Therefore, the Body of Christ was positioned in a NOW time for the release of wealth.

A NOW time

What is a NOW time? The Bible gives several different words for the word *time*. I wrote about these times in my book *Prophetic Intercession.*[1]

> The word *eth* in Hebrew is the same word as *kairos* in the Greek. Ecclesiastes tells us there is an *eth* time for every occurrence on Earth.... Powerful things will happen as we participate with the Lord at these specific times.

Wealth defined

Since this is a specific time for the release of wealth, what then is wealth? Is it only money or finances? Webster defines wealth as "much money or property or affluence."[2] In the Bible, one of the Hebrew definitions for the word *wealth* is *chayil*. Chayil is defined

---

[1] Barbara Wentroble, *Prophetic Intercession* (Regal Books, Ventura, CA, 1999), p. 93.
[2] Michael Agnes, Editor in Chief, *Webster's New World College Dictionary* (Macmillan USA, New York, NY, 1997), p. 1620.

as an army, wealth, strength, or a company of soldiers.[1] In other words, God has a strong army of spiritual soldiers rising with wealth and riches to fulfill God's Kingdom purposes on Earth. How awesome that you and I can be part of this great company of Kingdom men and women living at this time in history!

Reasons Christians don't desire money

How sad that so many followers of Jesus do not believe that Christians should have money. Many were taught that money is the root of all evil. Wrong! It is the *love* of money that is the root of evil (1 Timothy 6:10). The evil is rooted in the heart and not in the outward physical possessions. Some people take a vow of poverty believing that they will reach a higher level of spirituality. A person can have money and love Jesus at the same time!

Often, believers feel guilty if they have a desire for wealth. They believe they are carnal and not spiritual. They sense they do not have a grateful heart toward the Lord. After all, they may have more than their parents or grandparents had. Why can't they be satisfied with what they have rather than desiring more? How sinful and wicked their hearts must be!

Sometimes a person falsely feels they are filled with pride. They sense they are just wanting to be more successful than their friends or family. The person remembers Satan was filled with pride. Surely, the Lord must consider them very sinful and full of pride for wanting to have wealth!

---

[1] James Strong, *Hebrew Dictionary of the Old Testament* (MacDonald Publishing, McLean, VA), p. 39.

Good Samaritan had money

Many believers have never been taught biblical principles concerning money and wealth. Some have been told they should tithe. However, they have never understood God's purpose for the creation of wealth. Jesus explained by telling a parable about a man called the Good Samaritan. The Good Samaritan in the Bible must have understood the necessity of wealth (Luke 10:30-37). He found a man who had been beaten by robbers and lay in a ditch almost dead. Religious leaders and priests passed by the man. They were on their way from Jerusalem to Jericho, a city where priests and Levites lived. As spiritual leaders, they could not be distracted by such a dirty man. The wounded man surely was not on his way to a place of worship!

The Good Samaritan stopped to help the man. He felt compassion. The Bible tells us he bandaged the man, took care of him and then took him to an inn for the night. The next day, the Good Samaritan left money for the innkeeper to care for the man. He even promised to give the innkeeper more money the next time he came if he needed it to care for the helpless man. Jesus told His followers they should follow the example of the Good Samaritan.

Did you notice the Good Samaritan had enough money to care for the man who suffered beatings and theft from robbers? If he only had enough money for his own needs, he would not be able to help the man. If the Good Samaritan only had enough money to pay for his home and food on his table, he could not help the needy. He could not obey the Lord when God asked him to take care of the less fortunate. You and I are the same way. Jesus, in the parable, told us we are to do the same thing that the Good Samaritan did. We need wealth to obey the Lord and care for people who have suffered loss. It is not enough to be like the religious people that Jesus spoke about. It is not enough for believers to read their Bibles several hours each day, fill their schedules with weekly prayer meetings and pray for three hours each day. We must be people who have the resources to obey the Lord and fulfill His Kingdom purposes on Earth.

I grew up in a church that rarely talked about money. The pastor always reminded us that we needed to tithe. We also were asked to give into two mission offerings each year. Other than that, I don't remember ever hearing a sermon about the necessity of being a Wealth Creator.

Biblical understanding of wealth

God is uncovering truths in the Bible to His Church today. He is revealing Kingdom principles that have not been understood by this generation. One of these truths concerns the necessity and Kingdom function for wealth.

The New Testament records the Early Church bringing wealth and laying it at the feet of the apostles. These apostles had an anointing to attract wealth for Kingdom purposes. They did not gather wealth for themselves. They had a mandate from God to use the finances for God's purposes on Earth. Believers knew the character of these apostles. They knew the money would be distributed by the apostles under the direction of the Lord. They could trust the apostles to dispense the money according to God's heart.

> With great power the apostles were
> giving witness to the resurrection of
> the Lord Jesus, and abundant grace was
> upon them all. For there was not a
> needy person among them, for all who
> were owners of land or houses would
> sell them and bring the proceeds of the
> sales, and lay them at the apostles' feet;
> and they would be distributed to each,
> as any had need.
>
> Acts 4:33-35

Believers in the Early Church had a radical heart to help the needy. Some, not all, were even willing to sell their lands and homes to help their brothers and sisters in the faith. The result was no person in the church lacked. There was no poverty in the church!

God does not require every believer to sell their homes or property. However, He is calling us to have His heart for others. Maybe you have heard someone pray like this. "Lord, if You will put food on my table and a roof over my head, I will not ask You for anything more." That sounds very humble. Yet, I believe it is the most selfish prayer a person can pray. That prayer is about me and my family. It does not include anything for other people or God's purposes on Earth.

If people are going to be freed from human trafficking, drugs, abuse or many other horrible situations, it will take finances to give the help they need. Christians need to become Wealth Creators to help eradicate these evils from Earth. Some believers become Wealth Creators through their businesses.

Christian business or Kingdom business

I have heard many discussions about whether a Christian should own a Christian business or a Kingdom business. Often, people do not know the difference between the two. I do not believe one is right and the other is wrong. These businesses have different purposes. Both can be used by the Lord.

A Christian business is one that is owned by a Christian and hires other Christians to work in the business. Usually the employees should be believers. An example is a Christian bookstore. People come to the bookstore looking for answers to the challenges they are facing. They want books and other resources to help them find the answers they need. Believers with a working knowledge of the Bible and familiarity with available resources are the ones needed as employees. These Christian companies are not seeking to be elitists. They are merely employing believers to help them achieve their goals.

A Kingdom business is different from a Christian business. Kingdom businesses are owned by a Christian but can employ non-Christians. These employees are hired because they have the skills and abilities needed by the business. They are not hired because of their faith. The Christian owner creates a culture of honesty, integrity and other biblical attributes. The hope is that these non-Christians will see something in Christians that they want for themselves. However, the business is not created as an evangelism center. It is created to provide a Christ-like atmosphere for workers and to create wealth for Kingdom purposes.

Too many times business owners and marketplace people have felt they are second-class citizens in the Church. They are made to feel that they shouldn't desire to have a lot of money. If they have wealth, they may not love Jesus. What confusion this brings to the minds of businesspeople! They love making money. They love the challenges it brings. They love the fact that the money helps employees meet the needs of their families. They love having the finances to improve their cities, send missionaries to other countries, feed the poor and many other Kingdom projects. Yet, they feel guilty for desiring more money after hearing sermons that tell them not to desire the riches of this world.

I encourage people that they do not need to choose between loving Jesus and making money. They can do both! Make lots of money for the Kingdom. Love Jesus with your whole heart. You can do both at the same time!

Miracles or strategies?
Many Christians are waiting for the Lord to give them a miracle in their finances. They somehow picture God unzipping the heavens and dropping down a gold brick. They are at the altar every time there is a call for those needing a miracle from the Lord. I believe in miracles. I have experienced miracles in my life and my family. I pray for miracles. Still, miracles are the unusual. Wealth Creators may get a miracle on occasion. Most of the time, Wealth Creators need strategies from the Lord. They need the Lord's wisdom in their personal life as well as in their businesses. Strategies for the creation of wealth come from the Lord to business owners and marketplace people.

Having a Kingdom understanding of biblical economics is helpful when creating wealth. We will look at this in the next chapter. Get ready to become a Wealth Creator!

Practical Steps
1. What is a NOW time?
2. Give your definition of wealth.
3. Name two reasons that Christians believe they are not to have wealth.
4. Why does God want you to have wealth?
5. What is the difference between a Christian business and a Kingdom business?

The Promise
"I know the plans that I have for you," declares the LORD, "plans for welfare and not for calamity to give you a future and a hope."

Jeremiah 29:11

Decrees
- I decree that God desires me to be a Wealth Creator!
- I decree that I can hear the voice of the Lord for wealth creating strategies!
- I decree that I will love Jesus and create wealth at the same time!

CHAPTER 2

Revelation of Biblical Economics

In high school, I took several math courses. These courses included Algebra 1, Algebra 2, Plain Geometry, Solid Geometry, and Trigonometry. Not many students enrolled in these courses. They were difficult! I only enrolled in these classes because I planned to go into nursing school after graduation. I wanted to be sure I was prepared for the college courses I would take.

During those years of high-level math along with the normal math courses I took in elementary and middle school, I later realized something. We were never taught how to make a budget for our finances. We never were taught how to write a check, balance a bank account or read a financial report. All these skills are needed in real life for every individual. I do not remember ever needing the things I learned in the accelerated math courses.

How sad so many people have never been taught the elementary principles of finances needed for everyday living. How sad Christians usually have never been taught what the Bible says about economics. Often, Christians embrace anti-biblical philosophies that are in today's culture without any understanding of what God says about finances.

It is imperative that believers are taught biblical principles concerning finances. Otherwise, they will not be able to fulfill God's plan for their lives or His plan on Earth. The Bible is filled with revelation concerning God's desire for mankind to prosper in wealth. Wealth is needed to fulfill the Divine Mandate and the Great Commission.

God's first assignment for mankind
The first assignment God gave to man was to subdue the Garden and rule over it.

> God said, "Let Us make man in Our image, according to Our likeness; and let them rule over the fish of the sea and over the birds of the sky and over the cattle and over all the earth, and over every creeping thing that creeps on the earth."
>
> Genesis 1:26

The Garden was to be a training ground for God's first couple. If they were successful in that assignment, God would enlarge their territory and bring increase into their lives. However, we know they failed in their assignment in the Garden.

God, however, did not change His mind for mankind. The time came when He brought His Son, Jesus, into the world to make a way for following generations to fulfill that assignment. Jesus, in complete obedience to the Father, took back the assignment given in the Garden. He then handed it to all those who would follow Him.

> All authority has been given to Me in heaven and on earth. Go, therefore and make disciples of all the nations, baptizing them in the name of the Father and the Son and the Holy Spirit, teaching them to observe all that I commanded you; and lo, I am with you always, even to the end of the age.
>
> Matthew 28:18-20

Finances needed to obey God

For mankind to obey God's command, money would be necessary. Finances are necessary to subdue crime, human trafficking, drugs, infirmity, and many other evils in the world. You may even have a dream inside you for how God wants to use you for His purposes. It will take money to fulfill that dream.

I love the story of how a city was changed when God's people realized that God wanted to give them wealth to reform their city, Buffalo, New York. My friend, Al Warner, along with Pastor Tommy Reid, wrote the story in their book, *Create Wealth to Build God's Dream.*[1] A city that was described as in a death spiral became a city in Renaissance. These believers were obeying the Great Commission by discipling marketplace believers, including businessmen and governmental leaders. They believe that God gave them the ability to create finances and transform their city.

---

[1] Tommy Reid and Al Warner, *Create Wealth to Build God's Dream* (Kairos Publishing, 2015).

Changing a city or a region includes the understanding that Earth belongs to God. Earth does not belong to Satan. God put His people on Earth to manage Earth for Him. Man is a steward of Earth under the supervision of the Lord.

Scarcity rather than abundance

Although God released the ability to create wealth through multiplication and increase in mankind, Adam had to work harder after the Fall. He worked in an environment that was under a curse. Adam and the woman were not cursed. Yet, the land and serpent were cursed (Genesis 3:14-19). Because the land experienced a curse, Adam was denied many of the pleasures and benefits he previously enjoyed. Adam had to work harder for the ground to be productive. The Garden now looked like a place of scarcity rather than abundance.

Scarcity is a word that many modern-day economists use. These economists believe there is a limited supply of goods on Earth. They believe someone must sacrifice for others to have their needs met. The Bible gives a different picture of wealth for His people. He puts His creative ability in man so scarcity can be replaced with abundance. God has enough in His economy for every need to be met.

God's wisdom can create abundance

I love the way God used people in the Bible to take them from a place of scarcity to a place of abundance. Jacob was one of those people blessed by the Lord. Jacob had the history of being a crafty schemer. He went through many years of hardship as a wandering exile. Yet, God had a good plan for Jacob's life. Often, people today spend years enduring hardship. Sometimes they go from job to job or city to city looking for the blessings of the Lord. However, God still has a promise of blessing for His people. A prophetic promise from the Lord can give wisdom needed to change a person's situation from scarcity to abundance!

Jacob received wisdom and strategy to take the imperfect flock given him by his father-in-law and turn it into a flock that was of great value. "The man became exceedingly prosperous, and had large flocks and female and male servants and camels and donkeys" (Genesis 30:43). Jacob went from lack to prosperity! His past was not his potential. Neither is yours! God has promised blessings for His covenant partners.

Covenant promises of multiplication
God made covenant with Abraham. We are grafted into that covenant and have the capacity to receive the blessings promised by God to Abraham.

> I am God Almighty; Walk before Me and be blameless. And I will establish My covenant between me and you, And I will multiply you exceedingly...And I will establish My covenant between Me and you and your descendants after you throughout their generations for an everlasting covenant, to be God to you and to your descendants after you.
>
> Genesis 17:1-2, 7

I love the way Chuck Pierce explains the power of the Abrahamic Covenant to flow through the coming generations. That means the promises of blessings are for you, your children, grandchildren and for future generations!

> "The covenant that God made with Abraham was beyond any that had been seen or formed in the earth realm. This covenant was not limited to the confines of time or space. There are times when God limits the generational flow of blessings and curses for ten generations. However, this was not so with Abraham. Abraham's blessings were open-ended to all who would bless Abraham and his offspring as a nation."[1]

What a powerful promise! God promises to multiply through us. Kingdom citizens should always expect to increase. Jesus told a parable about servants that were given the opportunity to multiply and increase.

Parable of the talents

> It's also like a man going off on an extended trip. He called his servants together and delegated responsibilities. To one he gave five thousand dollars, to another two thousand, to a third one

---

[1] Chuck Pierce and Robert Heidler, *A Time to Prosper* (Regal Publishing, Ventura, CA, 2013), p. 12.

thousand, depending on their abilities. Then he left. Right off, the first servant went to work and doubled his master's investment. The second did the same. But the man with the single thousand dug a hole and carefully buried his master's money.

Matthew 25:14-18, MSG

The story tells about the man coming home from his trip. He spoke to the servants who increased his money. He told them it was good that they multiplied what he gave them. However, he rebuked the servant who merely held onto the money given him and kept it in a safe place. There was no increase for that money.

The master was furious. That's a terrible way to live! It's criminal to live cautiously like that! If you knew I was after the best, why did you do less than the least? The least you could have done would have been to invest the sum with the bankers where at least I would have gotten a little interest. Take the thousand and give it to the one who risked the most. And get rid of this "play-it-safe" who won't go out on a limb. Throw him into outer darkness.

Matthew 25:26-30, MSG

God has placed the DNA for wealth creation and multiplication inside every believer. Understanding the purpose of wealth keeps us focused on our Kingdom mandate.

Keep a Kingdom mindset

We are on Earth to steward Earth and to bless Earth. Believers are not only members of a nation but also members of God's kingdom. Wherever God places His people, He puts them there to be a blessing. Like Abraham, God wants you to release blessings on Earth. "I will make you a great nation, and I will bless you, and make your name great; and so you shall be a blessing" (Genesis 12:2).

Blessing a region or a nation usually takes finances. My friends, Woody and Melanie Blok, live in a small island nation. They have hearts to see Sri Lanka restored from poverty, sickness, idolatry, corruption and many other evils. They understand that God has given them a Kingdom mandate to be a blessing to their nation. They look for ways to bring increase and multiplication of their finances. They understand the necessity of money to change their nation.

Many young people in their nation do not have the skills necessary to get good jobs. The Bloks, along with their church, established a training center. They reach out into the community to people needing computer skills. They are training people with skills to prepare them for better jobs. These jobs give the workers an increase in their income. The finances help them break their families out of poverty.

The Bloks also oversee Shepherds Heart Childrens Home. They rescue abandoned girls from the dangerous streets in Sri Lanka. Without the availability of a safe home, many of these precious girls would be victims of sex-trafficking, drugs and other evils. A Kingdom mandate keeps Woody, Melanie and the staff at their church and ministry focused on the true purpose of wealth. None of them are hoarding finances for personal purposes. They find ways to multiply the finances that come into their hands for Kingdom purposes.

God does not have a problem with His people living in a good home and having their personal needs met. He merely wants believers to stay focused on the purpose for wealth creation. Wealth is needed for Kingdom expansion and Kingdom purposes. God owns the whole Earth. He needs people He can trust to manage wealth and be a blessing on Earth.

Remember God who gives wealth
Throughout history, we find people who have loved God and remembered Him during hard times. They pray for God to meet their needs. They pray for increase and multiplication of finances. Yet, often God is forgotten after wealth is obtained. Moses warned the Hebrews not to forget God after He blessed them.

> For the Lord your God is bringing you into a good land, a land of brooks of water, of fountains and springs, flowing in valleys and hills;… In the wilderness He fed you manna which your fathers did not know, that He might humble you and that he might test you, to do good for you in the end. Otherwise, you may say in your heart, "My power and the strength of my hand made me this wealth."
>
> Deuteronomy 8:7, 16-17

Understanding biblical economics is necessary for believers to move forward with courage for the creation of wealth. It is also necessary to stay focused on the purpose for the wealth. Always remember where God has brought you from. He brought each of us out of the enemy's bondage and into the freedom of the Spirit. That keeps our hearts remembering God placed us on Earth to represent Him and use wealth for His kingdom purposes.

Not all economic systems are designed for Kingdom purposes. We will explore some of those systems in the next chapter.

Practical Steps
1. Describe your understanding of biblical economics.
2. What was man's first assignment on Earth?
3. What is scarcity?
4. How does the Abrahamic Covenant affect believers today?
5. How does a Kingdom mindset keep a person focused on creating wealth?

The Promise
I am God Almighty; Walk before me and be blameless. And I will establish My covenant between me and you, And I will multiply you exceedingly... And I will establish My covenant between Me and you and your descendants after you throughout their generations for an everlasting covenant, to be God to you and to your descendants after you.

Genesis 17:1-2; 7

Decrees

- I decree that I am a manager on Earth for the Lord!
- I decree that I serve the God of abundance rather than scarcity!
- I decree that I am God's covenant partner!

CHAPTER 3

Doctrines of Socialism, Communism and Capitalism

I taught a course on the biblical principles of economics once a month for one year. I am not an economist. I am not an expert in economics. However, I am an American citizen who has traveled to many countries. I have seen the living conditions of people in communist or socialist countries. I also see the living conditions of people living in the United States.

I often think of one lady who lived under the communist, socialist system for many years. She is a woman pastor from Romania who enrolled in the biblical economics course that I taught. She received the teachings through CDs and other media sources. She was excited to learn biblical principles about finances. Each student was asked to return answers to questions from each of the sessions.

I was amazed at the answers the pastor sent to me! She began her answers by stating the following.

> I know that what I am hearing is true. I do not know this from teachings that I have had. I know it is true from

experience. I lived under the Communist rule from 1965 – 1980s.

Under that system, the people were very poor. We worked hard just to have enough food to feed our families. Because we were tired from working so hard, we didn't get involved in the political arena. However, the church prayed.

After the church prayed for many years, the Romanian Revolution of 1989 came. The old system came down! You asked what I intend to do with what I have learned in this course. I intend to tell everyone what I have learned. I never want my country to go back under that system again!

What a powerful testimony from someone who had lived under a political philosophy that keeps people in poverty, control and abuses! God never planned for His people to live under those oppressive situations. Yet, today we are hearing many people cheering for socialism and communism. Many of them do not understand the lifestyle of those trapped in these political bondages.

Communism
During the early 1990s, at the invitation of some young, firebrand Russians, I took teams with me to establish churches in several Russian villages. The country had recently come from under a communist

government into a more democratic government. I was appalled at the living conditions in those villages! Poverty and lack hung over the villages like a black cloud. I met doctors, visited hospitals and orphanages. The doctors could not understand why we thought they were anybody special. They received free education, because they were intelligent enough to go to medical school. However, they received the same income as other citizens.

The villages looked like what some people would call a "ghost town." The grass and weeds were several feet high. Everything was dirty and needed to be repaired. Bathroom facilities were crude or non-existent. Very few cars were available. Most people used public transportation. They were just learning about "privatization" of property. Up until now, property was owned by the government. To these people, this was the only life they knew. Now with miracle services and preaching the Good News about Jesus Christ, the people were excited and came alive. Entire villages came to the meetings, and their lives were transformed.

What then is communism? It is an economic system where the government owns the means of the production of goods. The government often tells the workers where they are to work. All property is common property. The actual ownership of property is by the community or the government.

The economic and social activity is controlled by a totalitarian state. Some people refer to that as a police state. Included in this system is the belief that there is a connection between the problems in society and an unequal distribution of wealth. Believers who support this idea believe that private property should be abolished. They also believe that a profit-based economy should be replaced with public ownership. Communism has as its basic belief that an elimination of private property ownership is the way to govern.

The theory of communism was developed by Karl Marx. He said this: "From each according to his ability, to each according to his need." His belief included the profits from business should be distributed to the workers and not go to the business owners. He felt that the community should take care of the needs of those who could not work. They would receive goods and services for whatever needs that they had.

Socialism

There is little difference between the purest forms of socialism and communism. During the 19th century, several writers interchanged the terms of socialism and communism. Some people refer to Vladimir Lenin for attributing the interchange of these terms.

Justin Haskins is a prolific writer and appears on various TV programs.[1] In an article on his website, Haskins stated that Lenin described socialism and communism as successive societies. These societies would evolve after the abolition of capitalism. He states Lenin referenced Marx with this philosophy. However, Haskins states that Marx never described his philosophy that way. Marx merely applied his principles to a society that embraces common ownership and democratic control. Marx never referenced these societies as being successive.

---

[1] Justin Haskins, https:// stopping socialism.com/2018/08/what's-the-difference-between-communism-and-Marx's-socialism.

The philosophy of socialism uses the government rather than the marketplace to distribute resources. Currently, the term "distribution of wealth" is heard in the political arena. The belief is that the working class of people are exploited. Because of this belief, the government should eliminate all class structure.

Socialism embraces the idea that every individual has the right to finances and goods to meet their needs. Therefore, individuals who own businesses are taxed heavily to provide the finances for the less fortunate. Several public services are also funded by high taxes. People work but the government provides free education, free healthcare and public transportation. Most public services are either free or provided at a low cost.

Often, socialist societies mandate vacations, number of work hours, sick time and other benefits for the worker.

Other beliefs in a socialist society is that the inhabitants of the world should share equally in resources and decision making. There are no national borders. There are no national banks and no national armies.

Communism and Socialism not part of God's economy

People who are not educated in biblical economics sometimes believe that God delegated everything to the state. No system of socialist or communist ownership is in God's administration. When the Bible mentions shared property, it was voluntary. There was a prophesied crisis mentioned in the New Testament (Luke 21). People were voluntarily selling property while they could They knew the prophecy that was prophesied about the coming crisis and sold property (Acts 4:33-35). This was not a mandate for all people in all generations. Land was promised to God's people as part of their inheritance. This is covered in the next chapter.

The characteristics that I mentioned as part of communist and socialist societies are only a few of the aspects in those beliefs. Capitalism is an economic system that can be traced back to biblical days.

Capitalism
The greatest difference between capitalism and socialism is the amount of government intervention in the economy. Socialist societies have more government intervention for the purpose of redistributing resources where they feel the need is the greatest. They feel the government should take the wealth from the rich and give to the poor. Capitalism is a system where inequality encourages innovation and increases economic development.

Capitalism fosters privately owned business ventures. Competition promotes prosperity. The individual owns the land and the business. The businesses can operate freely without leasing the land from the government.

Businesses that treat their workers fairly and pay good wages are usually successful. The good workers help the businesses to succeed. Both parties are working to prosper from their hard work and innovative developments.

In a capitalist society, government funding for social services is kept to a minimum. Health care is done in the private sector. Citizens purchase their own insurance.

Potential for success is valued in a capitalist society. Profit is the primary motive behind capitalism. I read a story about the advantage of capitalism in a poverty racked country. Before 1994, Rwanda was engulfed in a system of community workers. Everyone worked together but not much was happening. There was little growth in the economy of Rwanda. Then the country gave capitalism a try. Now, the economy is growing. The citizens realize that when they work hard, they are paid good salaries. The country embraced a theory called, Subjective Theory of Value. According to this theory, a person can trade their services or goods to another who values it more than they do. The person makes a profit, and the wealth of the country increases.

Biblical examples

The Bible has several examples of people who were willing to work for a profit and became wealthy. These people owned their own businesses. Jacob is an example of a man who received the strategy to compete and create wealth.

Jacob was willing to take the defective flocks as payment from his father-in-law, Laban. He gained strategy on how to produce better flocks. The time came when Jacob's flocks were large, premium flocks. He produced better sheep than his competition, Laban. Not only did Jacob increase in flocks but also in every other aspect of possessions.

> The man became exceedingly prosperous, and had large flocks and

female and male servants and camels
and donkeys.

Genesis 30:43

Abraham was another person in the Bible who
prospered in his own business. The time came when
Abraham's herdsmen and his nephew, Lot's herdsmen,
had a dispute. Not enough pasture was accessible to
sustain both men's flocks. The men agreed to separate
and go to different areas.

Lot chose the most fertile land. He wanted the
best that his eyes could see. "Lot lifted up his eyes and
saw all the valley of the Jordan, that it was well watered
everywhere – *this was* before the Lord destroyed Sodom
and Gomorrah – like the garden of the Lord, like the
land of Egypt as you go to Zoar. So Lot chose for
himself all the valley of the Jordan; and Lot journeyed
eastward. Thus, they separated from each other"
(Genesis 13:10-11).

Abraham agreed to dwell in land that was not
as fertile or as well watered. Abraham later has a
visitation from God. God made him rich, and now He
was giving Abraham a land to enjoy. He told Abraham
to lift up his eyes. Lot lifted up his eyes to what he
could see in the natural world. Abraham needed to lift
his eyes in faith to the promise of the Lord.

> The Lord said to Abram, after Lot had
> separated from him, "Now lift up your
> eyes and look from the place where you
> are, northward and southward and
> eastward and westward; for all the land

which you see, I will give it to you and
to your descendants forever."

Genesis 13:14-15

Abraham was willing to sacrifice prosperity for peace
between relationships. As a result, God gave Abraham
more than he lost. As a person pursues profit in
capitalism, character is vital. Greed and abuse of power
can tarnish the system. It is vital for businesses to
establish a Kingdom culture for capitalism to thrive. A
Kingdom culture is merely an environment where
people are treated with respect. Employees are
validated and compensated for their achievements.

God wants transformed people to go into
various spheres of society and bring transformation.
We recognize that other human beings are made by the
Lord. They should be treated as God's creation. Like
Abraham, a person must be willing to trust God in the
midst of loss and competition. God can give strategy
in the same way that Jacob received strategy to become
a Wealth Creator. The person must lift up his eyes to
the Wealth Creator for revelation, prosperity and
blessings. God can give enough for you and your
offspring to have an inheritance. We will look at that
in the next chapter.

I encourage you to continue studying the
policies of communism, socialism and capitalism.
Teach this to your children and grandchildren. Your
future and the future of generations depends on an
informed and vocal Christian community!

Practical Steps
1. Give your definition of communism.
2. Give your definition of socialism.

3. Give your definition of capitalism.
4. Which system do you prefer?
5. Why did you choose that system?

The Promise

Every plant which My heavenly Father did
not plant shall be uprooted.

Matthew 15:13

Decrees

- I decree every doctrine that is not of the
  Lord will be uprooted and destroyed!
- I decree that I live by the covenants of the
  Lord and His doctrines, not man's false
  doctrines!
- I decree that God is my source and not
  government!

CHAPTER 4

Biblical Principle of Inheritance

"My father just died. The funeral home requires thousands of dollars before they will bury him. I don't have the money for the funeral and don't know where to get it." The person ends the call with tears, frustration and grief.

I wish I could say that I only had one call like the one I just described. However, I have had many similar calls through the years. The person is grieving over the loss of a loved one. On top of that, they are now under great pressure to have the finances for the funeral expenses. How sad no preparation has been made for an inevitable event!

Unless Jesus returns, every person will one day face death. The Bible tells us there is a time to be born but also there is a time to die (Ecclesiastes 3:2). What will happen to our loved ones when that event occurs? What does the Bible tell us that we should do to prepare for that time? What does the Bible say about inheritance?

Inheritance for the faithful

Inheritance governs the passing of wealth and possessions from parents to children. The amount of wealth is not a prerequisite. The Bible is speaking of a Kingdom principle. God's plan for an inheritance is as old as the Garden of the Lord. The Lord placed Adam and the woman in the Garden as a training ground. They were put in the Garden to guard and subdue. If they were faithful to obey the Lord in this setting, God planned to send them forth to subdue the whole Earth.

Adam and the woman had an inheritance from Father God. Their Father owned the entire world. He has the irrevocable power to give His possessions to His children. Yet, the possession of the couple's inheritance was not automatic. They needed to prove themselves faithful to receive that inheritance. In other words, the promise was conditional.

Adam was God's firstborn earthly son. When he failed to obey and fulfill his responsibilities, he was disinherited. Adam, through his disobedience, put himself under Satan's rule. At that time, Adam lost his inheritance from Father God. After that, the only way to full sonship would be through adoption. Satan now had an opportunity to take possession of Adam's inheritance.

The Bible gives instructions that children should show themselves responsible before receiving their inheritance. In a very short time, too often the inheritance has been wasted on drugs, alcohol or frivolous living. Parents worked to save for their children, even though the children were irresponsible. The money never accomplished the purpose for which it was given. In fact, in situations like this, the money has been used to reinforce wrong and sometimes evil behavior. Like Adam, many of these people lose the inheritance that was prepared for them.

Satan the squatter

When Satan posed as the possessor of Adam's forfeited inheritance, he became a squatter; he is not the legal heir to the inheritance. I have visited several countries and saw how squatters live. In one country where I was visiting, I noticed tents alongside a river running through the city. I asked the driver of my car a question, "Why are those tents along the river?" "They belong to squatters," he replied. "What are squatters?" I asked. "They are people who move onto the land and live there. They do not own the land. They live there until the owner of the land evicts them," he responded.

That is what Satan did! He acted as if the whole Earth belonged to him. He tried to rule Earth. God did not give Earth, His creation, to a covenant breaker! Satan has not owned the world, and he is not able to rule Earth. He is an impostor who acts like Earth belongs to him. Believers must embrace the authority they have as children of God to evict the squatter from their inheritance! We will discuss how Jesus, the legal heir to Earth, came to restore the inheritance to God's children in Chapter 11.

Inheritance of land

Although Adam failed in his assignment, God continued to show His faithfulness to provide an inheritance for His children. Years later, He established a reward system for families that would participate in conquering the Promised Land. Families involved in the battle received an inheritance of land. Land that was given to these families were guaranteed permanent ownership. Because the land was given as permanent ownership, future generations were promised they would have an inheritance.

The conquering of the Promised Land was another training ground like Adam's training in the Garden. This was to be a headquarters for training to fulfill God's Mandate in Genesis 1:26-28.

> God said, "Let Us make man in Our image, according to Our likeness; and let them rule over the fish of the sea and over the birds of the sky and over the cattle and over all the earth, and over every creeping thing that creeps on the earth." And God created man in His own image, in the image of God He created him; male and female He created them. And God blessed them; and God said to them, "Be fruitful and multiply and fill the earth, and subdue it; and rule over the fish of the sea and over the birds of the sky, and over every living thing that moves on the earth."

Worldwide conquest was not to be achieved through carnal weapons. It was to be accomplished through ethics. Many religions use force, violence and control to gain followers. God desires for people to see His likeness and image in His children. As people see the true picture of the Lord, they want to be one of His adopted children.

The Bible records, once again in the Promised Land, mankind failed to obey the Lord. Satan remained as the squatter acting as if he was in charge of Earth. Yet, God's plan would not be stopped! The legal heir to God's Earth would come and restore the inheritance to a future generation of those who would follow the Lord!

Receive inheritance through faithfulness

Children must be taught biblical principles to prepare them for an inheritance. The Bible instructs parents to teach God's ways and His laws to their children. These children can grow up to be responsible adults who are able to receive an inheritance.

> These words, which I am commanding you today, shall be on your heart; and you shall teach them diligently to your sons and shall talk of them when you sit in your house and when you walk by the way and when you lie down and when you rise up.
>
> Deuteronomy 6:6-7

Too many parents wait for the youth leaders at church, the school systems or some other individuals to teach their children. A busy schedule is no excuse for not teaching our children the ways of the Lord.

I love the story of Susanna Wesley. She was the mother of 19 children. Susanna understood her responsibility to teach her children to walk with the Lord. She spent time with a different child each evening. Two of her sons have shaped the history of the Church. John and Charles Wesley are founding fathers of the Methodist Church. Susanna gave her children a godly inheritance more valuable than silver or gold. She also indirectly gave a godly inheritance to the entire world!

Susanna Wesley understood about faithfulness to God's law. Faithfulness was a requirement for inheritance in Israel. Each generation understood they were to serve the other generation. Children would take care of parents in their older years. Parents would save finances to help their children have enough money to do this. Success would come through serving one another.

Inheritance taxes

Inheritance taxes are often used to rob families of their inheritance. Those taxes tell people that the government is the legitimate heir for family inheritances. Government policies lead people to believe that families are not to take care of each other. Currently, 15 states and the District of Columbia have an estate tax, and six states have an inheritance tax. Socialist governing systems are the legal heir to inheritance. They have established laws that claim to take care of people from the womb to the tomb!

The government promises that older people can retire on Social Security or other government funded programs. Through these efforts, the government becomes a substitute for families. As government is used as a substitute for either the parent or child, the government becomes a biblically illegal heir to the inheritance. This becomes another attempt by Satan to gain the inheritance God planned for His children. He tried to steal the inheritance when Adam failed in his responsibility. He also failed to gain the inheritance when Israel failed in their assignment in the Promised Land. Today, Satan is again trying to gain the inheritance through government interference in the wealth of God's children.

I have talked with many people through the years who lost their inheritance of land and buildings. They usually lost it because they could not pay taxes on the land. The government acted as if they were the lawful heir to the land by demanding payment of taxes.

Serving others through giving is a key to wealth

Serving others is a powerful key to gaining an inheritance from the Lord. Jesus taught this principle to His disciples. "Sitting down, He called the twelve and said to them, 'If anyone wants to be first, he shall be last of all, and servant of all'" (Mark 9:35). The Jewish community understands this principle today. In the book, *The Jewish Phenomenon*, Steven Silbiger says that "Jews are the most philanthropic ethnic group in the country."[1] He continues by repeating a writing in the Talmud that clearly gives direction the Jews must follow. "You're only as wealthy as the amount you are able to give." He believes that in the Jewish community, giving is the key that has made them wealthy.

The Old Testament includes the same principle for giving to others. "Now when you reap the harvest of your land, you shall not reap to the very corners of your field, neither shall you gather the gleanings of your harvest. Nor shall you glean your vineyard, nor shall you gather the fallen fruit of your vineyard; you shall

[1] Steven Silbiger, *The Jewish Phenomenon*, (M. Evans, Lanham, MD, 2009), p. 35.

leave them for the needy and for the stranger. I am the Lord your God" (Leviticus 19:9-10).

Parents must teach their children the wise administration of money. They need to understand their responsibility to serve others through their finances and their service. An understanding of making a profit is necessary in the accumulation of wealth. Otherwise, the children can lose their inheritance. The children need a plan for serving their community and giving to the less fortunate.

Through the years, we have watched children set up lemonade stands in their neighborhoods. These children are learning to manage money, make a profit and provide for the need of refreshing for their neighbors. They are serving their community and creating some wealth for their future.

My friend, Doris Wagner, is a model for serving others. Doris, in her 80s, lost one leg through amputation, lost her husband through death and has several medical situations. Yet, Doris continues to serve others. She travels and teaches courses on deliverance. She also is faithful during the Thanksgiving and Christmas seasons to help the needy. At Thanksgiving, Doris helps cook and serve food to hundreds of homeless people. During the Christmas season, Doris and her daughter, Ruth Irons, ring the bells and collect money for the Salvation Army. They play Christmas music, hand out goodies to the children and create an atmosphere of joy for the shoppers. Usually, they collect more donations than anyone else in their community! Doris inspires all of us with her giving heart. She is leaving an inheritance to thousands as she joyfully serves the Lord and demonstrates His heart to everyone around her.

Inheritance for future generations

The Bible instructs parents to leave an inheritance in their families for future generations. "A good man leaves an inheritance to his children's children and the wealth of the sinner is stored up for the righteous" (Proverbs 13:22). God is a multigenerational God. He describes Himself as the God of Abraham, Isaac and Jacob. That is three generations. Proverbs tells us to leave an inheritance to the third generation – our children's children. That is a command from the Lord that Dale and I have embraced for years. Our heart's desire is to leave an inheritance for our children and grandchildren.

I am concerned when I see a bumper sticker on a car that reads, "I am spending my children's inheritance." That sounds like a very selfish thing to be doing! I am sure that the sticker is meant to be funny. However, it is not humorous when that happens to the next generation.

I make sure that not only my children, but my grandchildren are included in my will. I often tell parents to be sure they are leaving some sort of inheritance for their children and grandchildren. The amount is not important. The principle is important. If a person has only a small amount of finances, at least leave a small inheritance. Leave a legacy that tells your family you were willing to invest in their future. Set the example for them to follow. Your heart's desire is to leave an inheritance, as after you leave you are planning to enjoy your final inheritance in Heaven!

For some people, breaking a poverty mindset will be necessary for leaving an inheritance. We will discuss that in the next chapter.

Practical Steps

1. How did Adam lose his inheritance?
2. What was the importance of the Promised Land as a training ground for Israel?
3. Why was land important as permanent ownership in a family?
4. How can inheritance taxes cause a family to lose their inheritance?
5. How does serving and giving release an inheritance to others?

The Promise

A good man leaves an inheritance to his children's children and the wealth of the sinner is stored up for the righteous.

Proverbs 13:22

Decrees

- I decree that the "squatter" is evicted from my inheritance!
- I decree that my family will receive an inheritance!
- I decree that my family will serve the Lord and serve others!

CHAPTER 5

Breaking a Poverty Mindset

Dale and I love cruises! Our favorite place to cruise is Alaska. Maybe we enjoy our time there because of the wilderness, glaciers or peaceful atmosphere. Living in a big metropolis like the Dallas area gets a little hectic at times. We can relax and appreciate God's creation as we cruise the Inner Passage of Alaska! The gourmet food helps also!

I have met many people who are amazed that we do things like this. Some say, "That is my dream. Someday I want to take a cruise." Others describe a dream inside them that they long for. For some, the dream may be a new house, or a mission trip to another country or many other longings that are in their hearts. When I question these people as to why they are not experiencing their dream, they usually have one answer. *Money!* They don't have the finances needed to fulfill their heart's dream.

On one of our recent Alaskan cruises, we invited a group to join us. One lady told us that the cruise was a lifelong dream for her. How excited she was to do what she had always wanted to do. I gathered our group for a few mentoring sessions while we cruised. My goal was to help people define their purpose in life. During these sessions, Jennifer Waddell realized that her passion in life is to sing. She was amazed when she discovered the ship's personnel were auditioning passengers for a special musical event.

Jennifer auditioned and was one of eight people that were chosen on the entire ship. As she sang, *I Can See Clearly Now,* the people exploded in applause! Jennifer exploded in joy. She was living her dream! Jennifer knew she was stepping into her destiny.

Poverty mindset attempts to stop destiny

God has destiny for every individual. Too often, a poverty mindset attempts to stop the destiny from manifesting in a person's life. I once heard someone say, "Poverty is not a financial statement. It is a state of mind." A poverty mindset is not limited to people who are poor. Wealthy people can also have a poverty mindset. It is not a matter of financial resources. The mindset convinces the person that they don't have enough.

Poverty comes from a root word that means "small means" or "scarceness." A mindset of poverty keeps a person under a canopy of despair. Often the person feels they will never amount to anything. They don't have hope of ever getting a break. The person feels that others may get ahead, but life has them trapped in a place where they cannot escape.

Greek philosophers influence

How sad that people spend their lives in such a dilemma! How sad that many of these people are Christians. No one knows where the poverty mindset came from. Some people trace it back to the Middle Ages or medieval period. Some trace it to the Puritan movement. Others believe this mindset can be traced back to Greek philosophers. These philosophers influenced the Church, and the doctrines were taught in many churches, and continue to be taught in churches.

The Greek philosopher, Plato, taught that everything material is evil. Those who follow Plato's teachings believe this world is not the real world. It is only temporary and evil. That means your job, money and other material things are all evil. The real world is after this life. Real life, according to Plato, is in the spiritual realm. Hopefully, you will be able to step into heaven some day and enjoy the real.

During the Middle Ages, the leader, Constantine, selected Christianity as the best religion. No one is sure if he was a Christian. He merely felt Christianity was the best religion. He established it as the state religion. During that time, poverty vows were taken in the Church. Today, many people are still taking poverty vows!

Wrong use of scriptures instills a poverty mindset
Scriptures can be used to convince a person that they should not desire wealth. When a marketplace person hears teachings that suggest money is wrong, they struggle. After all, businesspeople are in business to make money. If they don't make money, the business closes.

A couple of scriptures that are used to cause a person to doubt God's will for them to have wealth are the following.

> A good name is to be more desired
> than great riches, favor is better than
> silver and gold.
>
> Proverbs 22:1

> Jesus said to His disciples, "Truly, I say
> to you, it is easier for a camel to go
> through the eye of a needle, than for a
> rich man to enter the kingdom of
> God."
>
> Matthew 19:23-24

Scriptures can be taken out of context and used as a weapon to keep believers from the will of God for their lives. Cults use scriptures to justify their deceitful beliefs. Jehovah's Witnesses distort the Scriptures. They use scripture to deny the deity of Jesus. I mention this in my book, *Removing the Veil of Deception*.[1]

> Here is a favorite verse of the
> Jehovah's Witnesses:

> > You heard that I said to you, "I go
> > away, and I will come to you. If you
> > loved Me, you would have rejoiced
> > because I go to the Father, for the
> > Father is greater than I."
> >
> > John 14:28

> The term *greater* in this verse refers to
> the Father's position rather than to His

---

[1] Barbara Wentroble, *Removing the Veil of Deception* (Chosen Books, Grand Rapids, MI, 2009), pp. 62-63.

nature. Jesus and the Father are one. But Jehovah's Witnesses use this passage to contradict the Nicene and Apostles' creeds, which state that the three persons of the Trinity are coequal and coeternal.

How sad that some churches also distort scriptures to teach that God does not want His people to possess wealth. Wrong thinking causes Christians to believe that God doesn't want them to have money.

Mission fundraising

I remember attending fundraising events in the past to support missionaries in various churches. We heard stories of missionaries who had sacrificed so much to share the gospel in foreign countries. We were told that people in those countries had very little food, poor sanitary conditions and no running water. These missionaries lived in poverty so that the people in those nations could hear the Good News of Jesus. The people involved in these projects to help people had hearts to advance the Gospel. They were simply taught an incorrect belief system.

These stories were followed by an appeal to raise money to support the missionaries. We were told that for the people in the countries to hear about Jesus, someone would need to sacrifice. Could we sacrifice one meal a week, we were asked? Could we sacrifice a cup of coffee each week? If we did not sacrifice, the poor people in those countries would end up in hell because they never heard about Jesus.

The idea of sacrifice comes from teachings of scarceness by economists. The belief is only a certain amount of goods is on Earth. If some people live in abundance, other people will suffer. What a myth!

The same amount of resources is on Earth now that was here in the beginning. Yet, the world is vastly different today. The reason is that mankind has taken resources and used them in creative ways to bring increase and multiplication. Man can create enough wealth to have plenty for themselves and missionaries. God is the God of more than enough!

Symptoms of a poverty mindset

I have mentioned several symptoms of a poverty mindset. There are many more. I am going to mention just a few more symptoms that hinder the creation of wealth.

Hoarding food and clothing

One symptom is the hoarding of clothes, food and other material possessions. I have heard about people who had so many bags of clothes in their garage that they couldn't get their cars inside. The person feels that *someday* they may need those clothes. Yet, they haven't worn any of them for the past 10-15 years!

Another person had so much outdated food in her pantry and freezer that most of it had to be thrown away. I remember people in an area where we lived years ago. Many were storing food that was guaranteed to last for 25 years. Garages and closets were filled with dehydrated food. Twenty-five years have passed. The food is no longer edible. What a waste of money and food!

Every person needs an ample supply of water and food to last a week or more for emergencies. Hoarding food and clothing in excess for many years is rooted in a poverty mentality. That mentality is the fear of not having enough.

King Solomon was the richest man in the world. Although he was very rich, he did not believe in keeping all the wealth for himself. "There is a grievous evil which I have seen under the sun: riches being hoarded by their owner to his hurt" (Ecclesiastes 5:13). The word *hoarded* is the same Hebrew word used in the Garden of the Lord. *Hoarding* and *keep* are the same Hebrew words in the Old Testament (*shamar* – Strong's # 8104). Adam was told to keep the Garden. The word *keep* meant that he was to watch over the Garden like a watchman. I wrote about this word in my book, *Prophetic Intercession.*

> The Hebrew word for keep is *shamar.* Zodhiates defines *shamar* as to restrain; to keep within bounds; to hedge around something as with thorns; to watch as a watchman of sheep or cattle; to guard as a prophet.
>
> Adam especially had a responsibility to recognize the preexisting boundaries of the garden (Genesis 2:15). He was then to guard the boundaries of the garden in the same way a watchman watches over sheep or cattle. Anything contrary to the Lord's will was not to be allowed in the garden.[1]

---

[1] Barbara Wentroble, *Prophetic Intercession* (Regal Books, Ventura, CA, 1999), pp. 85-86.

Adam was given the instruction to *shamar* as a good mandate. He was to be sure nothing outside the will of the Lord was inside the Garden.

You and I are to do the same thing. We are to *shamar* over our earthly possessions. Nothing outside the Lord's will should be among our possessions. That means when the Lord instructs us to be generous in giving and sharing with others, we are not to hoard our possessions.

A poverty mindset causes a person to hold on tightly to what they have. There is a fear of not having enough. Poverty is not a state of being. It is a mindset. A billionaire can think that a millionaire is in poverty.

Poverty mindset is a stronghold

A stronghold is a fortified place. In fact, stronghold is a military term. It has strong defenses against any resistance. If the stronghold is not conquered, a person will revert to it when under emotional pressure, in times of weakness or during difficulties. Conquering the stronghold of a poverty mindset is necessary. Otherwise, that poverty mindset will control the person when facing economic downturns, losses or when the person is emotionally drained. It will prevent them from moving forward to create wealth.

To become a Wealth Creator, a person must replace an old mindset of poverty thinking. I love the way The Passion Translation of the Bible exhorts us to develop this renewed mind.

> For although we live in the natural realm, we don't wage a military campaign employing human weapons, *using manipulation to achieve our aims.*

Instead, our *spiritual* weapons are energized with divine power to effectively dismantle the defenses *behind which people hide.* We can demolish every deceptive fantasy that opposes God and break through every arrogant attitude that is raised up in defiance of the true knowledge of God. We capture, like prisoners of war, every thought and insist that it bow in obedience to the Anointed One. *Since we are armed with such dynamic weaponry,* we stand ready to punish any trace of rebellion, as soon as you choose complete obedience.

2 Corinthians 10:4-6, TPT

This can be your season to break out of any poverty mindset that is hindering you from increasing and multiplying. Your parents or grandparents may have operated in a mindset of poverty. Ask the Lord to break it out of your bloodline. You can be the one to bring change and release faith for wealth creation into your children, grandchildren and future generations.

Sometimes debt will attempt to stop you in your goal for wealth creation. We will discuss that in the next chapter. Start now to celebrate the freedom you are coming into!

Practical Steps
1. What is a dream inside you that you have never stepped into?
2. How can you begin to move toward that dream?

3. How did the poverty mindset get into church doctrines?
4. Name one scripture that has challenged you in your desire for wealth.
5. What are two symptoms of a poverty mindset?

The Promise

He raises the poor from the dust and lifts the needy from the ash heap, to make *them* sit with princes, With the princes of His people.

Psalm 113:7-8

Decrees

- I decree that together, we the people of God, can eradicate poverty!
- We decree that together, with the help of the Lord, God's people will remove poverty across all economic levels, social status, religious identity, ethnic groups, and languages!
- I decree You, O God who sits on the throne, raise the poor from the dust and the needy from the ash heap. You make them to sit with princes and with princes of His people!

CHAPTER 6

Defeating Debt

Debt will rob you of your dreams! Often, when a person faces debt, they lose the dream they once knew. The future looks bleak. A person can feel helpless to change the situation. I have read stories of people committing suicide during the Great Depression of the 1920s.

The Great Depression is recorded as the worst economic downturn in the history of the industrialized world. Many people believe it began in the United States with the stock market crash in 1929. Others have different theories about what caused the Depression. On Monday, October 28, 1929, a record number of stocks were traded, and the stock market declined more than 22%. The situation worsened yet again on the infamous Black Tuesday, October 29, 1929, when more than 16 million stocks were traded. The stock market ultimately lost $14 billion that day.[1]

---

[1] https://socialwelfare.library.vcu.edu/eras/great-depression/beginning-of-great-depression-stock-market-crash-of-october-1929. Accessed March 6, 2019.

The economy had been great until that time. Investors had invested lots of money into stocks that were overvalued. As the Great Depression moved forward, unemployment increased, and debt was proliferating. People did not realize that banks were investing their money into unstable stocks. Businesses lost and had to go into bankruptcy. People found themselves in a situation where they could not find a job. Many Americans were forced to buy on credit, if they qualified. The number of foreclosures and repossessions rose steadily.

People were fearful of the future. They could not find a way out of their financial situations. A large increase in the number of homeless people was unavoidable. Bread lines and soup kitchens opened to feed people. Farmers couldn't afford to harvest their crops. They were forced to leave them rotting in the fields. At the same time, people were starving for lack of food.

Many other financial losses were occurring during this time. As a result, people lost their vision for their future. Pictures appeared in newspapers of people jumping out of high-rise buildings in order to commit suicide. Debt and financial failures were too much for them to live with. They felt that suicide was their only way to escape. Others who struggled lost vision for their future.

Debt and financial failure continue

Debt and financial struggles did not end when the Great Depression was over in the late 1930s. Many people struggled with fear of financial failure and debt for the remainder of their lives. They passed that fear of financial loss to their children and grandchildren. The survivors told stories around Thanksgiving dinners to the next generation about their experiences. Debt and financial failure didn't just rob one generation of their dreams. It robbed the following generations in their families of their dreams.

Since the Great Depression, debt has continued to enslave people. Although the economic situation is better, the slavery of debt continues keeping people in bondage to a Dream Killer!

National debt
The United States has a huge debt situation! Currently, the national debt for the most prosperous nation in the history of the world is over 20 trillion dollars! It is difficult to even imagine that amount of money! The national debt continues regardless of which political party is in control. Often, the nation merely prints money that has little or no value. As a result, money decreases in value. When a person notices the nation handling money in this way, it is easy to handle personal finances in a similar fashion.

Spending tomorrow's paycheck
Debt is spending tomorrow's paycheck today. It is a way of spending the future to gratify the present. As a person continues to sink into more and more debt, shame engulfs the person. There are times when debt requires the repossession of houses or cars. The person feels humiliated over their lack of finances.

The person can also feel they are a failure because of not handling their finances properly. Sometimes a person will say things like this.

> "I will never get out of this situation!"
> "Each time that I think that I am getting ahead, something happens, and I am back in debt."

Debt is part of a curse listed in the Bible.

> The alien who is among you shall rise above you higher and higher, but you shall go down lower and lower. He shall lend to you, but you shall not lend to him; he shall be the head, and you shall be the tail.
>
> Deuteronomy 28:43-44

> The rich rules over the poor, and the borrower becomes the lender's slave.
>
> Proverbs 22:7

Christians should learn to manage money rather than money managing them. God has a way to release you from being the lender's slave!

Keys to defeat debt
Here is the good news! You can defeat debt!

Key #1: Credit cards:
The goal of a credit card company is to keep you in debt. You continue to pay them so that they can make money. Paying the minimum amount monthly

on a credit card keeps a person in debt. The amount owed can cost untold amounts of money before the bill is paid.

Use the credit card for your advantage rather than the advantage of the credit company. Only put on the credit card the amount you will be able to pay off at the end of the month. I do this for our personal use and have a credit card for the ministry. We pay the entire amount owed on each of those cards when they are due each month. Free airline miles are the reward for using some cards. We do not pay any interest and have no credit card debt when we pay the bills each month. I like having the credit cards work for me!

I sometimes give gift cards or a certain amount of money to my grandchildren for Christmas, birthdays or scholastic achievements. They are learning they only have a certain amount of money. They can take the amount they have and learn to manage it. Usually, they think a long time before spending the money. They realize that their parents and grandparents are not teaching them entitlement. They are learning to earn their money. They are also learning to manage the money without incurring debt.

> The wicked borrow and pay not again (for they may be unable), but the (uncompromisingly) righteous deal kindly and give (for they are able).
> Psalm 37:21, AMP

Paying off credit cards puts you on a path to financial freedom. A good financial advisor is able to help you decide if you need to pay off one credit card before another, or if you should combine the debt on your cards to pay them off.

Key #2: Passion
A person must be passionate about defeating their enemy called Debt. To defeat this enemy requires steadfastness, confidence and vision. A passion for the elimination of debt ensures success. When a person has a vision for their life after debt is eliminated, they continue discovering the means to make it happen.

An athlete must always keep their eyes on the goal. If they allow distractions and look away from the goal, they lose the game. It is the same way when defeating debt. Keeping your eyes on the goal of being debt free helps to avoid any distractions or challenges along the way. The Lord continually gives you the strategy to help you meet that goal.

Time is not the problem in defeating debt. It may take one year, two years, five years to reach your goal. Your passion will keep you moving toward the goal as you realize you are farther along than you were when you began this journey.

Key #3: A vision that takes you from adversity to abundance
Vision remains a daydream unless you connect it with passion. When vision connects with passion, you begin to demand a better tomorrow than what you are experiencing today!

> When there is no clear prophetic
> vision, people quickly wander astray.
> Proverbs 29:18, TPT

Ask the Lord to give you a vison for your financial future. Allow that vision to take you from the adversity you may now be facing to the abundance God has for your life!

Key #4: Plan

Many people say that they need "more" in their lives. What does "more" look like to you? What will financial freedom do for your life? These are questions a person needs to answer before starting a plan to defeat debt. I once heard someone say, "When a person fails to plan, they plan to fail." Get help if you need to for developing a doable plan to get out of debt. Your future depends on it!

A mindset for prosperity is necessary to help shift a person into the blessings God has promised for them. Continue breaking the power of a poverty mindset when it tries to reappear and stop you in your quest as a Wealth Creator.

> O Lord our God, other masters besides You have ruled over us, but we will acknowledge and mention Your name only. They (the former tyrant masters) are dead, they shall not live and reappear; they are powerless ghosts, they shall not rise and come back. Therefore, You have visited and made an end of them, and caused

every memorial of them (every trace
of their supremacy) to perish.
                    Isaiah 26:13-14, AMP

The former tyrant master of Debt must not be
given resurrection power to arise and cause you
grief! That mindset has been broken and is dead.
Give life to your new mindset for wealth creation.

Begin now to develop a plan for eliminating
debt. We will discuss goals in Chapter 11. Let faith
arise to help you develop a plan to get out of debt
– forever!

Key #5: Purpose
Purpose defines who we are and why we are here.
Wealth alone never satisfies. A person must have
purpose for wealth. How does financial freedom
help you reach your life purpose?

I heard the CEO of a large company stress the
importance of our "why." He says we need to
know why we are doing something rather than
merely "what" we are doing. The "why" will keep
a person focused and passionate until they reach
their dream.

Your purpose requires action. What action can
you take today to move you from adversity to
abundance? Are you willing to overcome the
challenges you face as you move forward with your
plan to defeat debt? I wrote about this in my book,
Empowered for Your Purpose.

Several challenges are inevitable for
those who transition into a new place.
One of the challenges is that there must

be dissatisfaction with the present place. Those who are content where they are will not endure the difficulty of moving forward.[1]

Prospering in economic downturns

Defeating debt is crucial to becoming a Wealth Creator. The task is not easy. There are always times of crisis. The economy often changes. None of that should stop a person from continuing to press into their vision for defeating debt.

I read the story about the life of J.C. Penney. He began working for a chain of stores. He continued working there until he gained a large sum of money. He lost all the personal wealth he had gained after the stock market crash of 1929. He continued by borrowing money from his personal life insurance policy to meet the company payroll.

The difficulty from his financial loss and debt took a toll on his health. During that time, he became a Christian after hearing the hymn, *God Will Take Care of You*. Later, he trained a young man by the name of Sam Walton. He taught him how to wrap packages with a minimum of ribbon.

The J.C. Penney Department stores and Sam's Clubs are a result of someone who experienced financial loss and debt during an economic downturn. However, Penney put his faith in God to take care of him. He stayed focused on his goal. He turned his adversity into abundance as a Wealth Creator. You can do the same thing!

---

[1] Barbara Wentroble, *Empowered for Your Purpose* (International Breakthrough Ministries, Argyle, TX, 2018), p. 270.

You may be under the false notion that the market is saturated with so many inventions and good ideas. However, the world may be waiting for your innovation. Ask the Lord to give you a creative idea that can help you turn your adversity into abundance! We will discuss the war over wealth in the next chapter. You have the authority from the Lord to win the victory over that war!

Practical Steps
1. Talk about one story you have heard about the Great Depression.
2. How does national debt affect the citizens of a country and their personal debt?
3. Give your definition of debt.
4. What is the good and bad use of credit cards?
5. Discuss one of the keys to defeating debt.

The Promise
The alien who is among you shall rise above you higher and higher, but you shall go down lower and lower. He shall lend to you, but you shall not lend to him; he shall be the head, and you shall be the tail.

Deuteronomy 28:43-44

The rich rules over the poor, and the borrower becomes the lender's slave.

Proverbs 22:7

Decrees
- I decree I am the head and not the tail!
- I am rich in Christ Jesus and am not a slave to the lenders!

- I decree I have precious treasures and oil in my household!
- I decree I am generous and a generous giver!
- I decree I am one who seeks first the kingdom of God and His righteousness, and all these things will be added to me!

CHAPTER 7

War Over Wealth

My dad was in the Army and fought during World War II. He was a front-line machine gunner in the Battle of the Bulge. That was the bloodiest battle of the war. At the same time, it was also the battle that won the war.

My dad never talked much about the war. He didn't watch war movies. The memories were too painful. Occasionally, he mentioned that during the battle, every person in his troop would be killed except for him. He could hear the bullets as they whizzed by him.

This war was a global war that included over 100 million people from over 30 countries. The Battle of the Bulge was the largest, bloodiest battle in the war and the second deadliest battle during American history.

War is painful and leaves its scars. My dad suffered emotionally as a result of the war until he found Jesus during his latter years. After that, he was a changed man. He enjoyed peace rather than trauma, joy rather than sorrow and became a friend to all who knew him. I honor his memory for the sacrifice he paid to keep my family and this nation safe from the enemy.

We all owe a great debt of gratitude to those who serve in the military and the first responders who lay their lives down for citizens each day!

War to cross over into wealth

In the same way that there are wars in the natural world, there are wars in the spiritual world. For a person to become a Wealth Creator there will be a war to win. There will be a battle to cross over from a place of lack or barely enough to the place of wealth and abundance.

The Bible records the history of Israel at the time for them to cross over into their promise from the Lord. Former generations had lived in Egyptian captivity for 400 years. During that time, the Lord continued to promise the Hebrews a land filled with abundance and prosperity. The former generation looked at the challenges involved and refused to cross over. Now, a new generation arose that believed the Lord more than they believed their circumstances.

Often in families, former generations have lived in poverty or with a poverty mindset. They looked at their circumstances, their education or their abilities and decided that they were unqualified for wealth creation. God continues with His promise until a young generation arises that believes Him. You can be that generation!

Circumstances out of control

It is amazing that God chose a time to crossover when there was flooding, and everything seemed out of control. Why did He choose that time rather than a time of peace and an easier path to the next place? I believe He was desiring for His people to put their faith in Him and not their circumstances. He knows the perfect time for His people to crossover to their new place. It may be a time when circumstances in life seem to be the most impossible time. It is important to listen to the Lord and obey Him when He says it is time to move forward.

To cross over, God's people would need to have a Warrior Spirit. They would need to walk into the floodwaters of the Jordan before the waters parted. There were giants in the land that they would need to dispossess. They were provided with manna for food each day in the wilderness. When they crossed over, the manna would stop. Faith would need to be activated to receive the supply they needed. The Warrior Spirit would be necessary to stand against all opposing forces designed to keep them from the prosperity that the Lord promised.

A Violent Spirit

God has a Violent Spirit for those who enter His war for wealth. The enemy does not want God's people to prosper. He does not want you to cross over from lack and poverty into the wealth that He promised for His people.

> From the days of John the Baptist until now the kingdom of heaven suffers violence, and violent men take it by force.
>
> Matthew 11:12

Advancing God's kingdom requires force. God's people cannot advance without resistance and conflict. Satanic forces set up strong opposition to God's will for His children. Yet, God has a people on Earth with a Warrior Spirit. They will advance the Kingdom of God with a conquering force!

Never quit

This conquering force never quits! It never backs off! The only direction these people with a Warrior Spirit understand is forward! They are possessed by the energy and zeal of the Lord. They do not bow to religious and familial spirits of poverty. Their faith keeps warring for the promise of the Lord.

Warriors must also know who they can go to battle with. Not everyone has a warring spirit. Some people turn and run in the heat of battle. I wrote about this in my book, *Fighting for Your Prophetic Promises.*[1]

> We must know whom we can go to war with in times like this. Not everyone has a mindset to fight. Some people will run in fear in the midst of a crisis. It is okay to have lunch with these people. It is okay to be friends with them. You need to know, however, whom you can go to war with. Without the mindset of a warrior, a person is unable to fight for the victory of God's prophetic promises.

Mandate to create wealth

God has given His people a mandate to create wealth. It is an assignment by the Lord for His purposes to be

---

[1] Barbara Wentroble, *Fighting for Your Prophetic Promises* (Chosen Books, Bloomington, MN, 2011), pp. 184-185.

released on Earth. For the homeless people to be fed, the sex trafficking to be stopped, the nations to be discipled and many other Kingdom endeavors, finances will be required. The enemy will battle against these endeavors. He has people in bondage and wants to keep them there. God's people must keep their eyes on the purpose for wealth creation so they can be effective in warfare.

> You shall remember the Lord your God, for it is He who is giving you power to make wealth, that He may confirm His covenant which He swore to your fathers, as it is this day.
>
> Deuteronomy 8:18

God's mandate to create wealth will require spiritual authority to accomplish God's will. The authority needed is the power or right to give commands, enforce obedience, to act, or make final decisions. Those are spiritual assignments given to God's people for victory in their battles. We do this through intercession with decrees, proclamations and vocal commands.

Commanding poverty to be broken and the release of wealth to manifest move the person toward prosperity. Jesus demonstrated this when He was on Earth. He spoke to the storms to be still (Mark 4:39). He spoke to the barren fig tree to wither (Matthew 21:19-23). He commanded blind eyes to open (Luke 18:42). He did this so that His followers would know how to do the same thing and get the same results. He did not pray for the Father to look down and have mercy and change the situation. He knew He had the authority to be the voice of the Lord. He could speak to the situation and win the battle.

Speak to the resistance

> Jesus answered and said to them, "Truly, I say to you, if you have faith and do not doubt, you shall not only do what was done to the fig tree, but even if you say to this mountain, 'Be taken up and cast into the sea,' it shall happen."
>
> Matthew 21:21

In the war for wealth, a person must do the same thing that Jesus did. A person must speak to the resistance with great authority. We are agents of the Most High God. We are speaking His will into Earth by the power of the Holy Spirit. We speak and God's Spirit releases the power that brings it to pass.

Speaking to the resistance with boldness is necessary for breakthrough in the war. Boldness is God's weapon for defeating the enemy in warfare. Religion often infers that Christians shouldn't be bold. Many believers are taught that they should relinquish their rights and submit. No where in the Bible does it tell us that we are to give up our God-given authority and submit to the enemy! Believers should operate in the Spirit of Truth and see the enemy for who he is. A believer must discern the tactics of the enemy who does not want you to advance.

Timidity and intimidation

God has not given us a spirit of timidity, but of power and love and discipline.

2 Timothy 1:7

My life was controlled by fear and timidity before I experienced the infilling of the Holy Spirit. I thought that was merely the way God made me to be. It was not until the Holy Spirit revealed truth to me. He did not create me to be timid and shy. He created me to be bold for the Lord. He created you the same way. He made you to be bold and able to intimidate the enemy that is warring to keep you from creating wealth!

Intimidation is designed to keep you from your call as a Wealth Creator. A picture of how intimidation attempts to stop a person from God's will can be found in the Book of Nehemiah. Nehemiah was working to rebuild the walls and restore the gates of Jerusalem. Work was finally progressing despite the fierce opposition from others in the area. At one point Sanballat and Tobiah tried to intimidate Nehemiah in the attempt to stop the work.

> He spoke in the presence of his brothers and the wealthy men of Samaria and said, "What are these feeble Jews doing? Are they going to restore it for themselves? Can they offer sacrifices? Can they finish in a day? Can they revive the stones from the dusty rubble even the burned ones?"

Now Tobiah the Ammonite was near
him and he said, "Even what they are
building – if a fox should jump on it,
he would break their stone wall down."
Nehemiah 4:3

Tobiah was attempting to intimidate Nehemiah and his workers. Intimidation was the weapon of war designed to stop God's purpose in the Earth. The same weapon is used against believers today to stop God's will for their lives. Intimidation has a voice. It often says:

- *Who do you think that you are?*
- *What makes you think that you can create wealth?*
- *Others in your family tried to do this and they failed.*
- *The little amount of wealth that you make will soon be gone. Some crisis will come along and take what you have accumulated.*
- *Why don't you just give up and realize wealth creation is not for you?*

You have the authority from the Lord to stop fear, intimidation and any other weapon that the enemy uses to hinder your call as a Wealth Creator.

Battles are fought more than once

Battles are part of everyday life! Too many people expect to step into a season of peace, joy and smooth sailing. For most of these people, they will find themselves disappointed repeatedly. Reality tells us that life will have hardships, crises and economic downturns. The challenge in these situations is not to spend time hoping to get out of the situation. The real challenge is finding the strategy to win the battle you are now facing.

Margaret Thatcher is quoted as saying, "You may have to fight a battle more than once to win it." Ms. Thatcher was the first woman in European history to be elected as prime minister. She was the daughter of a grocer and battled through many difficulties before being promoted to the office of prime minister. Thatcher was nicknamed "Iron Lady." She received this name due to her unwillingness to compromise and her leadership style.

During her political career the nation experienced an economic recession. At this time her popularity decreased. She continued to battle through political challenges, unpopularity and economic problems in her nation. Thatcher was determined to win the battle and not give up. After several difficult years she received numerous awards and honorable titles. She understood that some battles must be fought more than once. She believed she had to always have the intent of winning the battle.

Your battle is a battle to create wealth. Yet, like Ms. Thatcher, you may need to fight the battle more than once to win it. Keep on persevering. Although you may have fought this battle before, do not stop now. Maybe this is the last time you need to fight this battle to win! You are in a war for wealth creation. You can win this war!

Alignment is another aspect of winning this war. We will discuss that in the next chapter. Keep warring for God's plan for you to be a Wealth Creator!

Practical Steps

1. How can a person cross over to a new place as a Wealth Creator?
2. Why does a believer need a Violent Spirit?
3. Who can you go to war with?
4. Why do you need boldness to speak to the resistance that is trying to hinder you?
5. What voice has intimidation used to try to stop you in creating wealth?

The Promise

You shall remember the Lord your God, for it is He who is giving you power to make wealth, that He may confirm His covenant which He swore to your fathers, as it is this day.

Deuteronomy 8:18

Decrees

- I decree wealth and health over me, my household and descendants!
- I decree I will serve the King of kings for His purposes!
- I decree that God has a plan for my life!
- I decree that with God's resources, I will fulfill His purposes on Earth!

CHAPTER 8

Alignment for Wealth Creation

I love stories about authentic people. One of my favorites is the story of Helen Keller. Helen developed an illness that left her deaf and blind when she was 19 months old. From that point, she described her life as living *at sea in a dense fog*.

A few years later, Helen's mother located 20-year-old Ann Sullivan and enlisted her as an instructor for Helen. That was the beginning of a 49-year relationship between Ann and Helen. Ann became Helen's governess and eventually her companion.

Ann's influence in Helen's life helped her learn to speak. Helen became a world-famous lecturer and author. She was actively involved with political issues and an advocate for people with disabilities. Her alignment with Ann Sullivan transitioned her from a place of lack to a position of abundant influence. Helen had the right alignment to propel her into her assignment in life!

Time of transition
You may be living at a point of transition in your life as a Wealth Creator. Like Helen Keller, it is your time

to transition from a place of lack to a position of abundance. When there is a transition, there is realignment and a cutting away of the old. Realignment gets us in the right place at the right time. During transition, it is imperative that we get rid of some old things that hinder us from the blessings God has purposed for our lives.

One of the hindrances may be alignment with some toxic relationships. A person must learn to deal with any toxic relationships in their life. Toxic relationships hinder a person from fulfilling their God-given destiny. Those relationships speak negative words, release painful emotions and keep life in a crisis mode.

Some relationships are better with distance and time. Put a little distance between you and that toxic relationship. Spend less time listening to those negative words. Refuse to live life in a crisis mode. God has better things for your life! Find the right alignment for your life!

Right alignment
Alignment is a word that can be defined as bringing parts together into proper coordination. Automobiles often need to be aligned so they function properly. Chiropractors and medical doctors often do procedures to align spines or bones. Proper alignment causes the vehicles, or the bodies, to function better and reach the capacity for which they were intended.

Right alignment releases a person into their destiny. A Wealth Creator needs to be aligned with those who see the potential and encourages them in their assignment. A right alignment will speak to the potential in you and not where you are today, or where you were in the past. It will cause you to function better and reach the capacity for which you were created.

Dr. Ron Cottle explains a few scriptures, he believes, that have erroneously interpreted the word *katartizo* as "equip" rather than the word "align." One of these scriptures is Ephesians 4:12. "for the equipping of the saints for the work of service, to the building up of the body of Christ."

Dr. Cottle explains the scripture this way.

> The overriding sense of this word group, then, is not to equip by supplying armor, or merely enhancing spiritual development (edifying). Rather, it is to put a thing into its appropriate position. Therefore, to establish or set, to ordain or commission, to fit or align, even to adjust or adapt are tasks much nearer to the essence of *katartizo* than to equip.[1]

To be successful as a Wealth Creator, you should find alignment with someone who will establish you in your appropriate position. In that position you can flourish and grow into your full potential.

Leave old place to get rightly aligned

I love the way the Book of Ruth in the Bible gives a picture of right alignment. Naomi, her sons and her husband, Elimelech, left Bethlehem during a time of

---

[1] Dr. Ronald E. Cottle, *Apostolic Alignment* (REC Ministries, Columbus, GA, 2017), p. 12.

famine. They looked for a place of prosperity. They arrived and lived in Moab for several years.

The new place did not turn out as envisioned. The sons died. Elimelech died. The place that was supposed to be a place of blessings turned into a place of disappointment and death. Naomi had to decide. Would she stay in the place of loss and death to her vision of prosperity, or go to the place of blessings? Wealth Creators often must make the same decision. Will they continue to do what they have done in the past or take a risk and go into a new place for the next season? Naomi made the decision to leave the old place. She had no guarantee for the future. She did not know where her finances would come from. She only knew that she could not continue in the old place.

Right alignment for the new season
Naomi's two daughters-in-law decided to go with Naomi to the new place. Later, only Ruth was willing to go. Not everyone wants to go where you are going. In fact, they often try to keep you in an old place. They want you to do what you have done in the past. Some people love for you to pray for them, so they receive peace. They love to spend time talking with you. They love all the things you do for them. There is only one problem. They don't want to go where you are going! A Wealth Creator needs to align with those that are going where they are going!

Ruth was determined to go where Naomi was going. She made a powerful statement about her covenant alignment with Naomi.

Ruth said, "Do not urge me to leave
you *or* turn back from following you;

> for where you go, I will go, and where
> you lodge, I will lodge. Your people
> *shall be* my people, and your God, my
> God. Where you die, I will die, and
> there I will be buried. Thus may the
> Lord do to me, and worse, if *anything*
> *but* death parts you and me."
>
> Ruth 1:16-17

Ruth came into right alignment with Naomi. She didn't consider the unanswered questions concerning her future. She didn't check her bank account to see if she had the finances to make the move. She only knew it was a heart connection. She was willing to stay aligned with Naomi through each difficult situation. Her future prosperity would be determined by having the right alignment in her life. If she had her alignment right, God would secure her future and her creation of wealth.

Not many fathers

A person can have many teachers and mentors. But, alignment with an apostolic mother or father is different.

> If you were to have countless tutors in
> Christ, yet *you would* not *have* many
> fathers; for in Christ Jesus, I became
> your father through the gospel.
>
> 1 Corinthians 4:15

Teachers and mentors are vital in our pursuit of wealth creation. A person may need to learn new skills, experience new ideas or broaden their list of connections. All of that is good. Spend time with men and women who have achieved goals and dreams similar to yours. Yet, the alignment with the right person to take you into your potential is still necessary. Be sure that person is someone who loves you and is looking out for your good. You don't want to be merely a name on someone's list. You need to have a heart relationship with someone who knows you and cares about your success.

I read the following quote from General Douglas MacArthur somewhere in the past. I wrote it down so I would always remember his powerful words.

> By profession I am a soldier and take pride in that fact. But I am prouder— infinitely prouder—to be a father. A soldier destroys in order to build; the father only builds, never destroys. The one has the potentiality of death; the other embodies creation and life. And while the hordes of death are mighty, the battalions of life are mightier still. It is my hope that my son, when I am gone, will remember me not from the battle but in the home repeating with him our simple daily prayer, "Our Father who art in heaven."

MacArthur was a powerful soldier. During a battle, when bullets are flying around, military soldiers remain loyal to their buddies. They will not leave a wounded solider on the battlefield. They have hearts that are connected. Those heart connections bring them through the battle. Our alignments should do the same thing.

Alignment without control

Alignment does not mean control. Right alignment does not control the other person. Your alignment should respect your free will. The person can offer advice and counsel, but you should be free to make your own decisions. The Lord does not control His followers. In fact, He issues stern warnings to those who do. In the Book of Revelation, the Lord speaks to the Church at Ephesus. "Yet this you do have, that you hate the deeds of the Nicolaitans, which I also hate" (Revelation 2:6).

The word Nicolaitans comes from a word that means "people conquerors." God wants His people to walk in joy and not defeat. Your alignment should help you walk in joy as you pursue your destiny as a Wealth Creator.

Doors open with right alignment

Aligning with Naomi put Ruth on a path to wealth. She started with nothing more than a heart alignment. She was willing to take a risk and move out of an old place and into unfamiliar territory. Naomi and Ruth were willing to step with faith into the unknown future. Their faith would put a demand on their circumstances to change. They were not making demands on God. They were demanding that financial lack would have to move aside so that wealth could be created.

After Ruth and Naomi arrived in the new place, an amazing door opened to secure their future. Ruth found herself in the field of Boaz at the urging of Naomi. Ruth found favor with Boaz. She later entered marriage with this very wealthy man. Without her alignment with Naomi, Ruth would never have possessed wealth.

Through Ruth, the line of David and ultimately Jesus came into the world. Ruth was a person outside the covenant root destined to receive from the Lord. She was a Moabite and not a Hebrew (Ruth 1:4). Moabites were not part of the bloodline to receive God's blessings. Boaz descended from Rahab the prostitute (Matthew 1:5). Together, they started a new bloodline destined to change the world. A door from the Lord opened to them that would change the world forever!

God chooses the least likely

God chose the most unlikely, least qualified people to create a bloodline to bring His Son into Earth! Let God use you to create a new bloodline in your family. He is choosing the most unlikely people today to create wealth for His kingdom purposes.

You may be one of the most unlikely people. Your family may not be the most spiritual, pious people in the land. You may have developed wrong alignments in the past. Yet, there is a fire burning in your heart. You desire a right alignment. You are willing to take a risk and go to where you have never been before. You are ready to start over in faith and demand a better tomorrow than what you are experiencing today.

Know who you are connected to and remain loyal during tough times! Right connections empower you to triumph in the battles of life. Wrong connections can maneuver you off course during those turbulent times. The power of remaining connected to those who are part of your destiny help you come through in victory and not defeat.

Creating wealth may involve your calling as an entrepreneur. We will discuss that in the next chapter. Like Ruth, you are starting on a journey to take you where you have never been before!

Practical Steps
1. Describe any toxic relationship that is in your life?
2. How will you deal with this relationship?
3. How do you plan to be positioned in a right alignment?
4. Describe any control issues that have affected you.
5. What area of your life do you feel makes you unqualified to be a Wealth Creator?

The Promise
If you were to have countless tutors in Christ, yet *you would* not *have* many fathers; for in Christ Jesus, I became your father through the gospel.
                                    1 Corinthians 4:15

Decrees
• I decree that God has given me God-ordained alignment!
• I decree the alignment in my life gives me the ability to be successful and effective in the Kingdom!
• I decree that I will multiply and experience the fulfillment of my purpose without ungodly control!
• I decree that my proper positioning helps to release my full potential!

- I decree I am blessed by the Lord God who made Heaven and Earth!

CHAPTER 9

Entrepreneurship

Wealth Creators see opportunities that others miss! My husband and I were visiting with my sister and her husband several years ago. They live in Texas along the Mexican border. We decided to go into Mexico, shop and have dinner. We parked close to the border for easy access, so we could return home easily later that day.

After a long day of shopping and eating wonderful Mexican food, we loaded into my sister's car. My brother-in-law pulled out of the parking lot and put on the turn signals for making a left turn to cross the border. A policeman was standing at the intersection directing traffic. He told Sam that he could not make a left turn. He must turn right and get in the line of traffic waiting to cross the border. We looked and saw cars lined up as far as the eye could see. We would be in that line for hours!

Suddenly a young boy around 10 years old appeared. He asked Sam if he wanted to get in the line of cars. Sam Rodio excitedly responded, "Yes!" The young boy held his arms up to the traffic as if he was a policeman. "Stop," he yelled to the ongoing traffic.

Traffic stopped, and the young boy waved us into the line. About that time, the policeman came to stop the boy from what he was doing. By that time, my brother-in-law had given that young boy more money than most of the boys on the street made in several days! The youngster saw an opportunity that others missed! I am not saying that breaking traffic rules is ok. I am just saying that Wealth Creators need to be alert when opportunities arise. They can create wealth in strategic times that others may not tap into.

Define entrepreneurs

God is issuing a clarion call to Wealth Creators who will advance His Kingdom on Earth. Often, those who respond to this call are entrepreneurs. An entrepreneur usually has the characteristics of a trailblazer or a pioneer. They love bringing change to their generation. Like the young boy in Mexico, they look for opportunities in their daily lives. Entrepreneurs start small and grow to achieve their goals. They have prophetic vision of what the future can look like.

According to U.S. Small Business statistics, in 2013 small businesses employed 56.8 million people, or 48.0% of the private workforce. Firms with fewer than 100 employees have the largest share of small business employment. Small businesses created 1.1 million net jobs in 2013.[1]

---

[1]

https://www.sba.gov/sites/default/files/advocacy/United_Stat es.pdf

Dr. Keith Johnson emphasizes the importance of vision in reaching a person's destiny. "When you don't have a sense of destiny or vision for the future, you tend to fall prey to the human tendency toward learned hopelessness and victimization."[1]

A person must have a vision for their future before they can possess it. An entrepreneur cannot allow life to bring whatever comes their way. They are put on Earth to bring change so God's will gets done on Earth as it is in Heaven. Too often we hear people say:

- *"I just want what God has for me."*
- *"Whatever the Lord has for me is fine."*
- *"No one else in my family has done this. Maybe this is not God's will for our family."*

If a person does not have a vision for their future, they will continue questioning whether they are in the will of God for wealth creation.

Entrepreneurs are anointed

In the Old Testament, when the time arrived for the Tabernacle of Moses to be built, God needed someone with prophetic vision. He chose a marketplace person to be in charge of the undertaking. The person had to be able to see spiritually what God wanted Him to see. Nothing like this had ever been built before!

God called on Bezalel, a marketplace person, to help build the Tabernacle. Bezalel was selected to be the chief artisan of the Tabernacle and was in charge

---

[1] Dr. Keith Johnson, *Leaders of Destiny* (Palm Tree Productions, Keller, TX, 2009), p. 2.

of building the Ark of the Covenant, assisted by Aholiab, a master of carpentry, weaving and embroidery. The first person in the Bible who was mentioned as "anointed" or "filled with the Spirit" was this marketplace person. Bezalel was known as the man who stood in the shadow of God. We need to pay close attention anytime a word or concept is mentioned for the first time in the Bible. The Law of First Mention gives a key for the fundamental understanding of other references to that word or concept. Bezalel was not a prophet or priest. He was a businessman. God has a call for businesspeople to arise and co-labor with Him for extending His Kingdom on Earth.

> Now the Lord spoke to Moses, saying, "See, I have called by name Bezalel, the son of Uri, the son of Hur, of the tribe of Judah. I have filled him with the Spirit of God in wisdom, in understanding, in knowledge, and in all kinds of craftsmanship, to make artistic designs for work in gold, in silver, and in bronze, and in the cutting of stones for settings, and in the carving of wood, that he may work in all kinds of craftsmanship."
>
> Exodus 31:1-5

Bezalel was an entrepreneur! He was called to create what had never been created before. He did not have a degree from a university or a trade school. He did not have a manual to read and show pictures of what needed to be created. God anointed him to be successful by filling him with God's Holy Spirit. He had the Spirit of God to give him prophetic vision to fulfill his assignment.

Classical view of God

Many people are fearful of taking a risk as an entrepreneur. They believe that if God wants something done, He will do it. If the Lord wants me to create wealth, it will happen. This belief will cause a person to wait on God for good things to happen. There is a fear of taking a risk and following the person's own desires and unctions. People sometimes sense they are being rebellious or carnal by following their own desires.

This belief comes from what is called The Classical View of God. That belief says that God predestined and controls all things. Your career, marriage partner, income, health, etc., are all predestined by God. The belief system causes a person to get rid of personal initiatives, so they don't "get out of the will of God."

I remember a time in my life when I battled with that belief system. I would sense the Spirit of God rising in me. I knew there were things He wanted me to do. However, I was fearful that the desires I sensed were my own flesh and not God's will for my life. Maybe I was carnal.

After struggling with these thoughts for years, I heard the voice of the Lord speak to me. "Barbara, you are trying to kill what I want to live." Wow! Immediately, my life came before my eyes. I realized how I would push down thoughts, ideas and plans. I was trying to kill the initiatives that God was trying to give me for the future. He was the One giving me those creative ideas. Yet, I was trying to kill what He wanted to live.

Immediately, I was set free! God's voice is the most powerful voice in the Universe! He wants to free His people from any hindrances that keep you from being a Wealth Creator. Your call as an entrepreneur will advance as you are directed by the Holy Spirit.

Entrepreneurs are problem solvers

Entrepreneurs are problem solvers. Creativity has been put inside God's people to be the answer to the world's problems. Throughout the Bible, we see examples of those that God used to address the problems of that day.

Joseph solved the problem of finances during a time of famine. His prophetic vision caused him to see the coming famine. He was able to develop a strategy that would provide food for the people during those difficult years. God gave him the ability to create wealth so he could serve others in a time of need. The creation of wealth was needed for a nation to survive years of famine and drought. Joseph operated in an entrepreneurial anointing to develop the enterprise that would save a nation.

Moses solved the problem of slavery by freeing God's people. Moses obeyed the voice of the Lord when he stood before Pharaoh in Egypt. God gave Moses the ability to create wealth by spoiling the Egyptians. The transference of wealth was used to provide for God's people as they traveled toward their Promise Land. It was also used to build the Tabernacle of Moses. The transference of wealth was necessary for a nation to be liberated from the captors and released into their promise from the Lord.

Nehemiah solved the problem of enemies coming into the city by building a wall and restoring the gates. He created wealth through the wisdom he spoke to the king. King Artaxerxes gave him the finances he needed for restoring the wall and gates of Jerusalem. The problem of invading enemy armies was solved by the entrepreneurial anointing that rested on Nehemiah.

Entrepreneurs press through difficulty
Your destiny, as an entrepreneur, is on the other side of your tight place. When you hit a bump or a slump in your business or ministry, it is time to keep the vision in front of you. Joseph had to remind himself of God's promise when he was in the pit or jail, or when he was falsely accused. He could not stop until he became a Wealth Creator and provided food for a nation.

Moses had to keep pressing through the difficult place when Pharaoh changed his mind and would not let God's people go. He could not stop until he gained the wealth of the Egyptians and freed a nation of slaves.

Nehemiah could not stop when he realized he was leaving a comfortable place as cupbearer to the king. He was going into enemy territory to restore a city for God's people.

I read the story of how Henry Ford pressed through a tight place. His destiny was on the other side of the tight place. Ford decided to produce the now famous V-8 engine. The idea was to build the entire eight cylinders in one block. The design was put on paper.

The engineers moved ahead with the idea. They really had no option since this was what Ford wanted. They had to press through this hard place if they wanted to continue on the Ford staff. After 12 months of pressing, nothing happened. They told Mr. Ford it was impossible to do what he wanted them to do. Ford told them to go ahead anyway. "I want it, and I will have it," he said.

The engineers continued in their seemingly impossible task. They had to stay focused and press again. Suddenly, they discovered a secret. Their determination and staying focused caused them to get through the place of impossibility! An entrepreneur must know what they want and press through the unbelief and impossibility.

Ford's destiny was on the other side of the tight place! The new V-8 engine produced a simple design. It resulted in the greatest production of V-8s to the masses. This invention outperformed all other competitors. It was an engineering marvel that was conceived years ahead of its time!

Influence capital in society

Your ability to solve problems gives you influence capital in society. A person gains influence when they serve others and serve society.

William Wilberforce was a British politician and philanthropist. One definition of *philanthropy* is: the love of humanity. A philanthropist promotes human welfare. It usually requires finances to accomplish the goal. Wilberforce lived in the late 1700s. He was a leader of the movement to abolish slavery. His good friend, John Newton, was a converted slave trader. He was also the author of the hymn, *Amazing Grace*. The two of them campaigned vigorously using their influence. Their goal was to abolish slavery throughout the world. It was a big goal, but they knew they had to find a way to solve the problem.

Their group was a small group of less than 20 people. Yet, the group was passionate. They were totally committed to their cause. They were committed to their faith and the purpose of their movement.

Decades later, the group saw the passing of the Slavery Abolition Act in 1833. The group had pooled their finances to create a supply of wealth. Their capital influence created powerful results! Wilberforce lived long enough to see the initial results of his dream. He died three days after the passing of the Slavery Abolition Act. The life story of Wilberforce is the story of an entrepreneur who dedicated his life creating wealth to be used for influence in eradicating human suffering. In 2007, the film *Amazing Grace*, a British-American biographical drama about the campaign against slave trade, was released. What an incredible legacy!

Entrepreneurs write their story

Ask yourself a question. *What is the story that you want written at the end of your life?* I remember a TV program when I was a child growing up. The program was called, *This is Your Life.* The host of the program would show pictures from the guest's life. Sometimes people the person knew years ago would surprise the guest and come on stage. It was so much fun to discover things about the person and hear what others would say about the guest. It was like living the person's life with them.

I have thought about that program many times. *What do you want people to say about you at the end of your life?* Do you want them to remember how you were willing to take a risk to make the world a better place to live? Do you want them to remember how you allowed your creative ideas to be used to help others have a better life? Do you want people to remember how you broke through poverty mindsets in your family and gave your children and grandchildren opportunities to succeed in life?

Go ahead and begin to write your life story now! Write how you shifted into God's promise to you for wealth. We will discuss that in the next chapter. You were created to be a Wealth Creator!

Practical Steps

1. Discuss an opportunity that you feel you missed in the past.
2. What is your definition of an entrepreneur?
3. Describe a problem you sense that you are called to solve.
4. What is influence capital?
5. What is the story you want written at the end of your life?

The Promise

Yours, O LORD, is the greatness and the power and the glory and the victory and the majesty, indeed everything that is in the heavens and the earth; Yours is the dominion, O LORD, and You exalt Yourself as head over all. Both riches and honor *come* from You, and You rule over all, and in Your hand is power and might; and it lies in Your hand to make great and to strengthen everyone.

1 Chronicles 29:11-12

Decrees

- I decree that it is my Father's good pleasure to reconcile things to me!
- I decree that I am an owner in the Kingdom of God!
- I decree that I take my responsibility as a steward to care for His things!
- I decree that my God is great, and His hand can strengthen me!
- I decree that God has a future and a hope for me!

CHAPTER 10

Giving Unlocks Wealth

Dale and I spent several years vacationing at the Summer Conferences at Christ for the Nations in Dallas, Texas. We were so excited to hear the speakers share what the Lord was doing in many nations of the world. One of our favorite speakers was a missionary to Mexico. He was a United States citizen and had given his life to reach villages all over Mexico.

This speaker had a motto that he lived by. *"Live to give!"* He made this statement frequently and with great passion. However, he did not merely say the words. He lived what he said. The school would buy a new suit for him when he came to speak. As soon as he returned to Mexico, he gave the suit to some pastor in a poverty-stricken village.

This missionary spoke words of faith to the people attending these conferences. He told them how the Lord always took care of him and met his needs. He kept doing his part by giving to others in need. As a result of his giving, God took care of him.

By the time this missionary finished speaking, the listeners wanted to give away everything they had for Kingdom purposes! Giving is a powerful key that unlocks wealth to those willing to obey the biblical principles found in the Bible.

Restoration of supernatural

Among other principles, the Lord is restoring truth concerning biblical finances today. The Early Church operated in many different principles; however, they are not always visible in today's Church. The Early Church embraced apostles, prophets, signs, wonders, miracles, angelic visitations, hearing the voice of the Lord, and many other supernatural operations. The New Testament is filled with stories about the power of God that affected the known world at that time. How tragic that so much of that understanding was lost during a time known as the Dark Ages.

Since the 1500s, God has been restoring lost truth. Beginning with Martin Luther, God has peeled back layers of darkness concerning the plan for His people on Earth. Among those truths is the biblical understanding of finances. Understanding and operating in biblical truth of finances unlocks supernatural creation of wealth and prosperity.

Prosperity measured by spiritual condition

All prosperity must be measured in comparison to the person's spiritual condition. A person should never take prosperity out of context with their walk with God.

> What will it profit a man if he gains the whole world, and forfeits his soul? Or what will a man give in exchange for his soul?
>
> Matthew 16:26

When a person listens to the Lord and obeys His instructions, the person is positioned to receive the blessings of the Lord. I love the way my friend, Robert Henderson, encourages God's people to receive the blessings of the Lord as they are faithful in giving.

The Lord showed me that the whole issue of determining the level of blessing that is coming into our lives, is the key to breakthrough. Breakthrough is when we go from one level to the next. We are to be going from faith to faith, glory to glory, and strength to strength. God made us to progress forward and experience ever-increasing dimensions of life and blessings. If we aren't, it is because we keep measuring out the same measurement and therefore getting the same thing back into our lives. If we want to have a "bigger life" and go to the next levels, we initiate it by stepping into a new measurement of giving. If we give, it will be given to us on the level that we apportion it out.[1]

Giving delivers from lack

I learned many years ago there are times when we must give our way out of lack. Dale and I have always been faithful to tithe. We were taught that principle as children in denominational churches. Although we

---

[1] Robert Henderson, *The Caused Blessing* (Robert Henderson Ministries, Colorado Springs, CO, 2007), p. 115.

were tithing, circumstances changed in our lives. We were in the midst of a major transition in life with three children in college. Circumstances changed that were beyond our control. Our income was reduced dramatically. We cut every place of spending possible. No newspaper, no cable TV, no money spent on clothes. We were desperate!

We knew that God's word is true. He promised blessings to those who serve him and obey His financial principles.

> I have been young, and now I am old;
> Yet I have not seen the righteous forsaken, or his descendants begging bread.
> Psalm 37:25

We believed that faith in God's word and obedience to His principle of giving would see us through the financial storm!

I cannot explain how God did it! All I know is that we continued giving although the amount may have been small. We knew if we stopped giving, we would cut off the supply line for God to bless. To quit giving was not an option! We continued tithing on the small income we had. We gave seed offerings and other offerings. God was faithful to bring us through a two-year financial storm!

I love receiving offerings in meetings! I love to teach on giving! I love to do this, because I know how the Lord wants to bless His people. I can do this with great confidence since I am a recipient of God's grace and mercy in times of need. I want others to experience the same freedom and blessing that I have received.

BARBARA WENTROBLE

Tithes to unlock wealth

The Bible teaches that the tithe is commanded by God. That means the tithe is not an option for believers. The first ten percent of income belongs to God. When a person does not give God His portion, the person robs God.

> Will a man rob God? Yet you are robbing Me! But you say, "How have we robbed Thee?" In tithes and offerings.
>
> Malachi 3:8

Some people believe that tithing is an Old Testament principle. These people believe it is "under the Law." They do not believe that tithing is for New Testament believers. Yet, we see Abraham giving a tithe to Melchizedek 500 years *before* Moses received the law. "To whom also Abraham apportioned a tenth part of all *the spoils*, was first of all by the translation *of his name*, king of righteousness, and then also king of Salem, which is king of peace" (Hebrews 7:2).

We, as New Testament believers, are connected to Abraham by covenant. Therefore, we are in line to receive the same blessings as Abraham received. "If you belong to Christ, then you are Abraham's offspring, heirs according to promise" (Galatians 3:29).

Jesus affirmed the principle of tithing in the New Testament. "Woe to you scribes and Pharisees, hypocrites! For you tithe mint and dill and cumin, and have neglected the weightier provisions of the law; justice and mercy and faithfulness; but these are the things you should have done without neglecting the others" (Matthew 23:23).

Jesus was reminding the Pharisees and Sadducees that they were correct in tithing. However, they should not neglect the right spirit while they were being obedient to the word of God.

Tithing releases blessings

There is a blessing attached to each type of giving. The Bible tells us the tithe belongs to the Lord. When we obey the Lord by tithing, a blessing is released to our lives. He opens the windows of Heaven and pours out amazing blessings. He also rebukes the devourer.

> "Bring the whole tithe into the storehouse, so that there may be food in My house, and test Me now in this," says the Lord of hosts, "if I will not open for you the windows of heaven, and pour out for you a blessing until it overflows. Then I will rebuke the devourer for you, so that it may not destroy the fruits of the ground; nor will your vine in the field cast its grapes," says the Lord of hosts.
>
> Malachi 3:10-11

A believer is motivated to tithe by a heart of love toward the Lord. The person loves God and wants to honor Him with the portion that belongs to Him. Others may look for excuses not to tithe, but to the people who give from a heart of gratitude to the Lord, they cannot help but tithe. They have a heart to obey

God. They also enjoy the benefits and blessings that come through the windows of Heaven into their lives!

First Fruit giving

The Bible gives us another way to give and to receive blessings from the Lord. We see a picture of this in the Old Testament. During the time of the early harvest, the priests would cut a portion of the barley and wave it before the Lord (Leviticus 23:17-20). The first portion was given before the harvest matured. The priests were operating in their faith in the Lord. They were doing a prophetic act to demonstrate their trust in the Lord for the increase and multiplication of the harvest.

> Honor the Lord from your wealth, And from the first of all your produce; So your barns will be filled with plenty, And your vats will overflow with new wine.
>
> Proverbs 3:9-10

The Bible does not tell us how much we are to give. We only know that as we give a generous amount to the Lord, we receive generous blessings.

Blessings of First Fruit

The blessings of first fruit offerings is the promise that everything that comes after that is blessed by the Lord. "If the first piece of dough be holy, the lump is also; and if the root be holy, the branches are too" (Romans 11:16). There is a difference between first fruit giving and tithing. The Bible sometimes mentions both types of giving to distinguish the difference.[1]

Tithes are given *after* the harvest comes in. The person gives a tenth portion of the income. First fruit occurs *before* the harvest. It is a generous offering given by faith before the harvest comes in. The blessings of First Fruit are that everything coming in after that is blessed of the Lord! When we give First Fruit offerings, the Lord promises that there will be an abundance of blessings from the Lord! Our barns (financial accounts) will be filled to overflowing and our vats (lives) will be filled with new wine!

Alms giving to meet a need

Alms giving is offerings given to man and not to God. "Every time you give to the poor you make a loan to the Lord. Don't worry – you'll be repaid in full for all the good you've done" (Proverbs 19:17, TPT). A person has pity on the poor, gives to meet a conference budget or donates to some humanitarian cause. These are all examples of alms giving. The return on the alms giving is the lowest amount of return. Yet, the Lord will return blessings dollar for dollar.

That is one reason I never take an offering in a conference to "meet the budget." I prefer another type giving so the people can reap a greater harvest. *I do believe in giving alms!* Dale and I give alms frequently. We have hearts for the less fortunate. We want to see groups have the finances to fulfill their vision. Our hearts are filled with compassion for the needy. We merely give other types of offerings for the greater return.

---

[1] Nehemiah 12:44

Blessings from alms giving

The blessings from alms giving is that the Lord will repay you in full for all you give. He repays dollar for dollar anytime you give. The motivation for this type giving is compassion. Hearts of compassion desire to help the less fortunate. There is a desire to see others delivered from the tight financial place they are in. Be sure to always include alms as part of your giving!

Seed giving brings increase

The final giving, I will mention is seed giving. Seed giving is potential fruit. I like to compare seed giving to an apple tree. I love looking at apple orchards in eastern Washington state. Each tree began with one small seed. Over time, the tree grew. It produces hundreds of apples each year. Those apples produce thousands of seeds each growing season. Year after year, the tree continues growing apples that are filled with thousands of seeds. That is a picture of seed giving!

Seed giving brings the greatest return of all the types of giving. A person cannot give seed offerings until they first tithe. Seed giving only starts after the first 10 %. Seed giving begins with 11% after the tithe.

I remember giving a seed offering at church several years ago. I wrote a small check for $50. This was after my tithe. I told Dale that the check was worth $5,000. That was my faith level for the check. The next morning after Dale arrived at work, he was called into the office. He was told that the company had just created a new job. They wanted to offer the position to Dale. With the new position they were going to increase his annual salary by $5,000. I am sure the seed offering opened the door for increase and multiplication in our finances!

Blessings of seed giving

The motivation behind seed giving is great faith! The person gives into vision for increase and multiplication of their gift. God blesses the person with increase like the apple tree's multiplication. The blessings of seed giving brings the increase needed to create wealth. It gives the person an opportunity to build the vision they have from the Lord.

Seed giving should be done with joy and gratitude to the Lord. Seed giving is not done out of compulsion but from an opportunity to plant in good soil for a great harvest.

> Now this I say, he who sows sparingly shall also reap sparingly; and he who sows bountifully shall also reap bountifully. Let each one do just as he has purposed in his heart; not grudgingly or under compulsion; for God loves a cheerful giver.
>
> 2 Corinthians 9:6-7

Giving seed offerings releases abundant blessings from the Lord for increase and multiplication!

Wealth Creators are givers

People who do not know the Lord have learned the principle of giving for increase and multiplication. Many companies donate ten percent of their profits to charitable organizations. They realize the benefits they receive as the company's revenue multiplies.

Greed and hoarding have no place in the life of God's Wealth Creators. They love giving! They love receiving the blessings of the Lord. They love giving to the less fortunate in the world. They often set goals for greater blessings to flow through their hands. We will look at that in the next chapter. Keep the blessings of God flowing through you to bring change into the world. You are advancing the Kingdom!

Practical Steps
1. How does the Bible speak about the spiritual life of a person regarding prosperity?
2. Describe the meaning and blessings of the Tithe.
3. Describe the meaning and blessings of First Fruit giving.
4. Describe the meaning and blessings of Alms giving.
5. Describe the meaning and blessings of Seed giving.

The Promise
Now this I say, he who sows sparingly shall also reap sparingly; and he who sows bountifully shall also reap bountifully. Let each one do just as he has purposed in his heart; not grudgingly or under compulsion; for God loves a cheerful giver.

2 Corinthians 9:6-7

As for the rich in this present age, charge them not to be haughty, nor to set their hopes on the uncertainty of riches, but on God, who richly provides us with everything to enjoy. They are to do good, to be rich in good works, to be generous and ready to share, thus storing up treasure for themselves as a good foundation for the future, so that they may take hold of that which is truly life.

1 Timothy 6:17-19

One gives freely, yet grows all the richer; another withholds what he should give, and only suffers want.

Proverbs 11:24

Decrees
- I decree that I am a cheerful giver!
- I decree that I will obey the Lord in financial giving!
- I decree that I will find life, righteousness and honor by pursuing righteousness and faithful giving to our God!
- I decree that my trust for financial blessings is in the Lord!

CHAPTER 11

SMART Goals for Advancing

I read a story that reminds me of people who don't have clear direction in their lives. The story went like this.

> The pilot made an announcement on the plane's intercom. "I have some good news and some bad news. The bad news is that we lost one engine and the direction finder. The good news is we have a tail wind. Wherever we are going, we will get there at 600 miles per hour."

Often, people tell me how busy they are. In the same conversation, they tell me they are not sure where they are going. They are busy with lots of activity. But they are not sure if they are accomplishing anything meaningful in their lives.

Sometimes people are like the plane I mentioned. They merely fly through life without any specific direction. These people have no direction, no energy and merely drift through life hoping they end up in a good place. Where do you want to be in five years? In ten years?

New Year's resolutions

Goal setting is vital for Wealth Creators. Yet, goal setting cannot be done the way many people are attempting by listing some objectives at the beginning of the year. In doing so, they hope to have reached their objectives by the end of the year. They create what is called New Year's Resolutions. Those resolutions may include getting out of debt, losing weight or writing a book. They start out strong and determined to accomplish those goals. Usually by the end of three months, many of the resolutions have been forgotten. Circumstances in life have crowded out their resolutions and goals. They justify discarding these resolutions by convincing themselves they are too busy. Some think or say, *This is not the right time for this to be accomplished.* Maybe they are attempting something impossible for their lives. Lots of excuses!

Goals are the guidelines that help a person's dreams come true. Goals help a person plow through the difficult and seemingly impossible situations in life. They keep a person moving forward during times when it would be easy to quit. A Wealth Creator must have the attitude that quitting is not an option! Goals help a person know how to direct their energies rather than staying busy and accomplishing nothing. Energy is then spent moving the person forward in their dream.

Past is not potential

Winners make goals; losers make excuses![1] Refuse to make excuses and blame others for your current situation. A victim mentality convinces a person that other people and circumstances outside their control has created the situation. Other people do not control your destiny! You, with the Lord's help, can overcome any situation that is attempting to stop you in becoming a Wealth Creator.

Refuse to allow your past to keep you from moving forward. Your past does not determine your future. It does not determine your potential. You cannot change your past, but you can change your future. God promises a good future for His children. The Bible promises believers a hope and a future (Jeremiah 31:17).

Goal setting releases power

Goal setting empowers a person to accomplish their dream. The impossible dream becomes possible when a person is committed to reaching their dream. I remember watching TV as the United States put the first man on the moon. United States leaders set a goal and reached that amazing goal in only eight years!

Bill Gates was nearly broke in 1975. He became America's richest man in 1995. These individuals, along with many others, refused to allow circumstances to hold them back from their dream. They set goals for a new future. You can do the same thing!

---

[1] Anonymous.

SMART goal setting

I love the acronym for goal setting that many leaders use. SMART goal setting is a powerful way to create direction when focusing on becoming a Wealth Creator. SMART is an acronym for the five elements of specific, measurable, achievable, relevant, and time-based goals. It is a simple tool used by businesses to go beyond the realm of fuzzy goal-setting into an actionable plan for results. Dr. Keith Johnson writes about the importance of written goals in his book, *The Confidence Makeover*. He says that a dream tells a person *where* they want to go. A goal tells the person *when* they want to get there. A strategic plan tells the person *how* they are going to do it.[1]

Specific in goal setting

The first part of goal setting that should be considered is being *specific* with your goals. Nehemiah is a great example of a man who was specific in accomplishing his dream for the restoration of Jerusalem. He had to do more than look at the ruins of the city with his physical eyes. He needed spiritual eyes to see the possibilities. He also needed to pray specific prayers to realize when he received specific answers. Too many people pray, "Whatever you want, Lord, is fine with me." They never know if their prayers are answered.

What do you want to see happen when you are creating wealth? Do you want to be debt free in two years? Do you want to bring in an extra $20,000 annually to finance a Kingdom project? Be specific in your goal.

---

[1] Keith Johnson, *The Confidence Makeover* (Destiny Image Publishers, Shippensburg, PA, 2006), p. 224.

Measurable results

The ability to measure results keeps a person on track and moving forward. My bookkeeper gives me monthly, quarterly and annual financial reports. I can see where I am financially in comparison to where I was last year, last quarter or last month. By doing this, I can make any adjustments I need to make so I can meet my financial goals for the year. The results I see on these reports are measurable.

Often, I hear people say they want change in an area or situation. They tell me that when they prayed, the atmosphere changed. They believe that ensures the answer to their prayer. What happens when the atmosphere changes? Does the crime rate change? Did the person receive healing? Did the economy change? You need a way to measure results when you set goals for wealth creation.

Attainable results

When asking people to define the vison for their lives, some people have lofty dreams. Some of these visions are probably not attainable during their life time. One answer people give to my question is, "I just want the whole world to love Jesus." That is a great goal. However, it is most likely not to happen soon. Others may say, "I want my entire family to be happy." Once again, that may not be an attainable goal. People have a free will. Prayer can help soften their hearts, but each person must decide if they are going to live in happiness and joy.

Another person may say their goal is to be debt free in six months. The person may be in debt for $50,000 and making minimum wages. Meeting that goal is probably not attainable in six months. It may require a longer period. What is an attainable goal you can make as you press forward as a Wealth Creator?

Relevance in goal setting

A person must decide the relevance for the goal they are setting. How does this goal help you move toward becoming a Wealth Creator? What will happen if you get out of debt? What will having a larger savings account do for your peace of mind?

Joseph, in the Old Testament, stored grain for seven years (Genesis 41). He did not do this merely to have a large storehouse. He didn't do it to prove he was richer than other people. He stored grain, because it was relevant to his goal. His goal was to be a provider of food for a nation in a time of future drought. Storing grain became relevant to meeting that goal.

Relevance is vital as a person sets goals for becoming a Wealth Creator. This aspect keeps the person from activity that is unproductive in reaching their goal.

Time-specific goals

Goals need to be time-specific. How long will it take to accomplish your goal? It is amazing how distractions can keep a person from accomplishing their dream. There will always be emergencies and unexpected events in life. These detours can keep a person from ever crossing the finish line for their dream.

I write books, travel to speak in meetings, do several conference call events monthly, oversee an international network of leaders, involve myself with children and grandchildren, am a wife and keep household details in order. In other words, I am an extremely busy person. For me to write books, I must have time-specific goals. I hear people talking about attempting to write a book for 4 to 10 years!

I must decide when I want my book published when I start writing. Every step of book writing goes on my calendar. I detail the steps on my calendar in the same way that I schedule a speaking engagement or a birthday party. By having a specific time to release my book, I can always do what I need to do to reach a time-specific goal. I make sure that I include times for contingencies. Life never happens the way we think that it will.

Abraham waited 25 years for his goal to have a child. I am sure it seemed like an eternity for him and his wife. But God! The Lord is faithful when we do not give up along the path of wealth creation.

Be willing to break down your time-specific goals into doable segments. I break down writing chapters for a new book into the amount of time it takes to write a chapter. I then put each chapter on the calendar. These doable segments keep me motivated as I see the progress I am making. I have the energy to keep pressing forward and meet my deadline.

What is a time-specific goal you have for creating wealth? Will it take six months, a year or two years for some goal that you have? Whatever time it takes, you will be farther along than you are today. You didn't get the way you are overnight. It may take longer than overnight to reach your goal. However, you will be closer to fulfilling your call as a Wealth Creator!

Failure to set goals

There is no condemnation in failing to meet your goals. The failure is in refusing to set goals. How sad that some people settle for life the way it comes. They embrace whatever life brings their way. Everyone gets knocked down at some point. Finances change, relationships change. Jobs change. There are lots of unpredictables in life.

Failures and devastating circumstances do not define who you are. The only people who fail are the ones who get knocked down and stay down. A person can only fail when they refuse to get up and go again.

Everyone makes mistakes. Yet, your mistakes do not determine your value in life. You are a unique individual who was created with great potential. Do not allow the financial mistakes made in the past stop you from advancing toward a fresh start.

Put things in their proper perspective. You are on a journey you have never travelled before. Your life stands in front of you. Pull yourself up and start again. Refuse to allow discouragement to stop you.

A new beginning

Start to create wealth with whatever you have. Don't waste time complaining about what you don't have. Don't despise small beginnings. Everything begins small. You began as a small embryo in your mother's womb. Every flower began as a small seed. Wealth is often created from a very small initial investment. When the person is faithful to continue investing small amounts, compound interest can grow a meager amount of money into a sizeable fund.

Use the seemingly small ability that you have in the same way. Let this be a season when you find creative ways to use your talents. Set SMART goals for a new beginning. As you use whatever you have, it will increase and continue to grow.

Now, ask yourself. *What do I have that seems so small?* How can I use this small beginning to start creating wealth that can grow and become great? Be willing to start with what you have today. Watch and see your small beginning turn into a Jubilee for your life! We will discuss that in the next chapter.

Practical Steps

1. What is a New Year's resolution that you failed to keep in the last year?
2. How have you overcome a victim mentality?
3. What is one SMART goal you have for creating wealth?
4. What do you use to measure the results of your goal?
5. When will you set your goal for Wealth Creation?

The Promise

My son, do not forget my teaching, but keep my commands in your heart, for they will prolong your life many years and bring you peace and prosperity.

Proverbs 3:1-2

Whatever you do, do your work heartily, as for the Lord rather than for men, knowing that from the Lord you will receive the reward of the inheritance. It is the Lord Christ whom you serve.

Colossians 3:23-24

Decrees

• I decree that as I plan, God will give strategies!

- I decree that I am not a procrastinator!
- I decree that with the help of the Lord, I can accomplish my goals!

CHAPTER 12

Path to Becoming a Wealth Creator

Such a cute movie! We laughed, sometimes cried and loved watching a movie with such a great message. Although I do not often watch movies, I loved this one. "Angel in the House" is the story of an angel coming to the home of a couple. He stayed for awhile and helped to transform their lives. One of the ways he helped them to transition was in the area of finances.

The man in the movie, Alec, was facing a financial downturn in his business. The angel discovered some old toys in the man's office. After inquiring about the toys, Alec said they were toys from the past. The company built those toys years ago. They were now sitting on shelves because no one wanted to buy them. That was one of the reasons for the financial situation they were in.

The angel found a new strategy for selling the toys. He repackaged them for a new look. Suddenly, the business was booming with the Surprise Packages filled with old toys! The businessman discovered that he already had in his hands what was needed to become a Wealth Creator.

What is in your hands?

You are probably like Alec in the movie. You may already have in your hands what you need to begin your journey as a Wealth Creator. I remember the Lord reminding me of this truth years ago. I wanted to start a biblical learning institute. "Where will the money come from to do this?", I asked the Lord. He asked me a question. "Barbara, what do you have in your hands?" I looked around the office. Suddenly, I realized that I already had what I needed to begin. I could rearrange the office to have more space. Dale went to a wholesale company and bought folding chairs. We bought a large whiteboard. We started the institute with a very small investment.

Look around you at what you already have. Is there a way for you to begin as a Wealth Creator with what you have in your hands? Too often people wait for some unknown, large amount of finances, a big building or some other costly investment before they begin.

Moses was asked the same question. God was sending him to fulfill his destiny and spoils from the Egyptians for a wealth transfer. Moses was concerned that he would not be able to accomplish the mission God was sending him on. The Lord spoke to Moses to assure him of success.

> The Lord said to him, "What is that in
> your hand?" And he said, "A staff."
> > Exodus 4:2

The Lord was assuring Moses that he already had what he needed to be successful in his assignment. So do you!

Jubilee
God is positioning His people on a new path. Believers can move toward their destiny. They can go from a place of lack and begin to create wealth for Kingdom advancement. We see a picture of this in the Old Testament.

God's plan was that every 50 years the land must be returned to the legal heir of the original family. This appointed time was called Jubilee. Jubilee would give families the hope of restoration when they lost land. Jubilee was God's plan to restore the lost inheritance. Slaves would be set free. It symbolized the year of full deliverance. Jubilee represented the restoration of all things.

Jesus fulfilled Jubilee
How sad that there is no record in the Bible of Jubilee ever being fulfilled and celebrated. Thousands of years later, Jesus came on Earth to announce His ministry as the fulfillment of Jubilee! Remember, we discussed the squatter sitting on land that God promised for His children. He would sit there until the legitimate heir came to claim his inheritance. When the legal heir arrived, the squatter could be evicted from the land.

Jesus made a profound statement when He announced His arrival to fulfill Jubilee.

> The Spirit of the Lord is upon me, and he has anointed me to be hope for the poor, freedom for the brokenhearted, and new eyes for the blind, and to preach to prisoners, "You are set free!" I have come to share the message of

> Jubilee for the time of God's great
> acceptance has begun.
>
> Luke 4:18-19, TPT

The word *prisoner* literally means *prisoner of war*. Many people are prisoners of the war for wealth creation. The good news is that Jesus came to set you free from your imprisonment! He made a powerful announcement to the poor.

> "You don't have to be poor!"
> "You have an inheritance!"

Jesus fulfilled the terms of Isaiah 61. He was proclaiming that a title deed transfer had occurred. The title deed for Earth was transferred from the deceased Adam to God's incarnate Son. Jesus was declaring that He was the legitimate Son who had come to claim His inheritance. Satan, the squatter inheritor, was put on notice that the heir had come for His inheritance! His inheritance was the entire Earth!

Believers given keys
Jesus did not keep the inheritance for Himself only. He was ready to share it with His followers.

> This is the rock on which I will put
> together my church, a church so
> expansive with energy that not even the
> gates of hell will be able to keep it out.
> And that's not all. You will have
> complete and free access to God's
> kingdom, keys to open every door; no
> more barriers between heaven and

earth, earth and heaven. A yes on earth
is a yes in heaven. A no on earth is a no
in heaven.

Matthew 16:18-19, MSG

The victory for Jubilee was at the cross. I love the way
my friend, Dr. Patti Amsden describes this conquest.

> The victory was at Calvary, not during
> a three-day demonic torture session in
> hell. Christ's victory was a legal victory,
> not a pugilistic struggle. Therefore,
> God held the keys of hell.[1]

Adam lost the keys after his disobedience. The keys
were then held by God until Jesus came and fulfilled
Jubilee. God gave the keys He was holding to Jesus.
The keys were not transferred from the devil to Jesus!
They were given by Father God to the Son, the rightful
heir, the Lord Jesus! Jesus then turns to those who
would follow Him. He offered the keys to every
believer.

I will give you the keys to the kingdom.

Matthew 16:19

Key of identity for Wealth Creation
What are some of the keys that Jesus has for Wealth
Creators? One key is the key to a new identity. As a
Wealth Creator, you cannot be who you were in the
past. Negative voices, painful experiences and defeats
can attempt to give you a false identity. Those

[1] Dr. Patti Amsden, *Ekklesia* (Patti Amsden Ministry,
Collinsville, IL, 2016), p. 37.

experiences are not who you are. They are merely events. God made you as a unique individual. No one else has your fingerprints or your DNA. Even snowflakes are created with an individual identity.

You were chosen for greatness. Get in the Presence of the Lord and allow Him to tell you who you really are.

> Oh yes, you shaped me first inside, then out; you formed me in my mother's womb. I thank you, High God – you're breathtaking! Body and soul, I am marvelously made! I worship in adoration – what a creation! You know me inside and out, you know every bone in my body; You know exactly how I was made, bit by bit, how I was sculpted from nothing into something. Like an open book, you watched me grow from conception to birth; all the stages of my life were spread out before you, the days of my life all prepared before I'd even lived one day. Your thoughts – how rare, how beautiful! God, I'll never comprehend them! I couldn't even begin to count them – any more than I could count the sand of the sea.
>
> Psalm 139:13-18, MSG

What a powerful scripture that lets believers know their true identity in the Lord!

Great leaders in the Bible sometimes needed a new identity to fulfill God's call on their lives. Joshua was a warrior under the leadership of Moses. Later, he became the leader for taking God's people into the Promised Land. He needed a new identity as a leader and not just that of the warrior he had been in the past. You will need to receive a new identity for your call as a Wealth Creator. Remind yourself of what God's word says you are. Rehearse your name in front of the mirror each day if you need to. Whatever it takes for you to receive a new identity, just do it!

Key of coaching for wealth creation
No person has all the revelation, all the wisdom or the perfect ability to hear God for themselves. The Lord created us to need each other. That need may include a coach to partner with us for our success. Coaching is a key that can bring you from where you are to your God-given potential.

In the Old Testament, David coached 400 men. They were an outcast group who were discouraged, in debt and discontented (1 Samuel 22:1). David's mighty army went from a position of insignificance to a position of being significant in advancing God's kingdom on Earth.

Coaching provides keys that unlock people's minds, hearts and dreams. Coaching breaks you out of the limitations of the past and releases you into the limitless possibilities of the future. Look for someone who sees the potential in you.

I read that the greatest athletes usually come from small, unrecognized schools. They are like a big fish in a small pond. But surprisingly, they are able to lead their obscure school to a high profile championship. Athletic scouts are able to see the potential in a person. They are willing to invest in the person, so they become better not perfect. A few people can be perfect, but most people can become better in pursuing the path to wealth creation.

A coach will do that for you. A coach is not someone who controls you. The purpose of the coach is for impartation. The coach may only be for a season. Let the season with a coach be one that shifts you to a new place. Go ahead and invest in your future as a Wealth Creator. Partner with a coach and see where God will take you!

Key of intercession

A powerful, necessary key for wealth creation is intercession. Praying opens the heavens for a person to receive strategy and instructions from Heaven. The key for God's direction in creating wealth is for the person to be receptive to the voice of the Lord. The person operates in a new level of hearing. I wrote about this in my book, *Council Room of the Lord, Accessing the Power of God.*[1]

> In a time when so many people are experiencing hopelessness in their situation, God has promised access through a door of hope. This door will bring expectation for a better future. It will cause the person to regain confidence that their prayers will produce results.

---

[1] Barbara Wentroble, *Council Room of the Lord, Accessing the Power of God* (International Breakthrough Ministries, Argyle, TX, 2018), p. 14.

God is a loving father and desires to speak to His children. As a believer, you can hear the voice of the Lord.

> My sheep hear My voice, and I know them, and they follow Me.
>
> John 10:27

In intercession, the Lord will speak wisdom, strategy or revelation for creating wealth.

Some individuals or businesses have a team of intercessors. They realize that they need exponential power in prayer to accomplish their mission. These intercessors war against spiritual darkness. They command every dark power of resistance to move aside. They pray for spiritual ears to open and hearts to receive the word of the Lord.

Find several people who love you enough to pray for you. Ask them to intercede for you to fulfill your mission as a wealth creator. Use the key of intercession to unlock your future.

Key of connections

Get around people who want you to get to your next level of wealth. Spend time with people who are positive. Get around those who will celebrate you and encourage you.

We live by encouragement. Our deepest human craving is to feel appreciated. Without a sense of approval, we die on the inside. People usually put forth more effort and try to do a better job when they live under a spirit of approval than under a spirit of criticism.

Sam Walton was an entrepreneur and businessman and is best known for founding the retailers Walmart and Sam's Club. He was a man who devoted his life to encouraging others. He and his wife worked to put the same principles into their own children. Walton once said:

> Outstanding leaders go out of the way to boost the self-esteem of their personnel. If people believe in themselves, it's amazing what they can accomplish.

Power to make wealth

Many Christians too often rely on God creating some supernatural miracle and dropping wealth into their hands. They hear testimonies of how God met a person's personal needs; however, these individuals may end up only surviving and not multiplying for increase. Most people seldom hear testimonies about God giving strategies for wealth creation. Ask the Lord to give you a mindset that agrees with His promise for your life.

> You shall remember the Lord your God, for it is He who is giving you power to make wealth, that He may confirm His covenant which He swore to your fathers, as *it is* this day.
> Deuteronomy 8:18

My prayer for you is that this will be a time when you transition from where you are to where you want to be! Your present position is not your destiny. You are in transition and God's blessings are in front of you. Don't miss the best that God has for you! Become the Wealth Creator that God made you to be!

Practical Steps

1. What do you have in your hands to take your first step toward wealth creation?
2. What was one benefit of Jubilee?
3. What is an old identity that you need to change?
4. Describe the benefits of having a coach.
5. What is a scripture that promises God's people that they can create wealth?

The Promise

For it was the *Father's* good pleasure for all the fullness to dwell in Him, and through Him to reconcile all things to Himself, having made peace through the blood of His cross; through Him, *I say*, whether things on earth or things in heaven.

Colossians 1:19-20

Decrees

- I decree the celebration of freedom for a Jubilee in my life!
- I decree that I am free from depression and the spirit of slavery!
- I decree that restoration is in my life for possessions and for relationships!
- I decree that I will experience multiplied increase of blessings from my labor!

- I decree that I will experience deliverance, safety and exponential blessings in my life and the lives of my children and descendants!
- I decree that I receive the blessings of Jubilee!
- I decree that my faith in God brings about these results!
- I decree that it is not by my power or my might but by His Spirit!
- I decree that my faith in God brings blessings into my life!

About the Author

Barbara Wentroble leads an apostolic network and a strategic alliance of visionary leaders globally. She is a strong apostolic leader, gifted with a powerful prophetic anointing. Ministering with cutting-edge teaching and revelation, a powerful breaker anointing is released. Giftings and anointings in ministers, business leaders and individuals are activated for the purpose of fulfilling their destiny.

Barbara conducts leadership conferences to emphasize releasing God's transformational power in cities and regions. She has been involved in the global prayer movement since the 1990s and travels around the world.

Recently Barbara launched the online course: *How to Become a High Level Prophetic Intercessor.* She is the author of twelve books. These books include *The Council Room of the Lord: Accessing the Power of God, Accessing Your Prophetic Gift, Accessing God's Healing Glory; Prophetic Intercession; Praying With Authority; Removing the Veil of Deception; Fighting for Your Prophetic Promises; People of Destiny, and Empowered for Your Purpose.*

Barbara is founder and president of International Breakthrough Ministries (IbM) and Breakthrough Business Leaders (BBL). She and her husband Dale reside in Lantana, Texas. They are parents of three adult children and eight grandchildren.

Barbara's contact information:

Website: www.barbarawentroble.com

Email: info@barbarawentroble.com

Mailing Address: P.O. Box 109, Argyle, Texas 76226

Office Phone: 940-735-1005

Empowering Resources

Get Connected: Align with Barbara Wentroble
Phone: 940-735-1005
Email: info@barbarawentroble.com

Order Books, Products and Join Our Free
Monthly Spiritual Growth Trainings:
Go to website: www.barbarawentroble.com
- Free Monthly Mentoring Calls
- Prayer Conference Calls
- Breakthrough Business Leaders gatherings:
  Local onsite meeting in Corinth, Texas or
  Facebook Live Broadcast

Complete travel and special events schedule:
www.barbarawentroble.com

High-Level Intercession Training
How to Become a High-Level Prophetic Intercessor
Online Training for Individuals or Groups
Two Levels: Ten sessions each level
Includes manual for each level

Breakthrough Books
Prophetic Intercession
Unlocking Miracles and Releasing the Blessings

Praying with Authority
How to Release the Authority of Heaven

Fighting for Your Prophetic Promises
Receiving, Testing and Releasing Your Prophetic Word

Removing the Veil of Deception
How to Recognize Lying Signs, False Wonders, and Seducing Spirits

Empowered for Your Purpose
Keys to Unlock Your Future

Breakthrough Products
Breakthrough Anointing Oil
Council Room Anointing Oil

Council Room of the Lord Series
These books are to encourage believers to press into the Lord's Council Room to receive a Holy Spirit empowerment that is ushering in a powerful movement for the Kingdom of God. If you would like notification about future book releases in the series, please inform the office.

Books in Series
- The Council Room of the Lord: Accessing the Power of God
- The Council Room of the Lord: Accessing Your Prophetic Gift
- The Council Room of the Lord: Accessing God's Healing Glory

Made in the USA
Columbia, SC
01 May 2019